A HAUNTED LAND

Ireland's most atmospheric sites
and strange stories of presences and hauntings.

Bob Curran is an educational psychologist at the University of Uster, Coleraine. He also works extensively in community education and with adults in return-to-education schemes. His community-based approach links him with the history and folklore of many areas all over Ireland. His interests are broad-ranging but are focused especially on history and story. He has written several books, including *A Bewitched Land: Ireland's Witches*, *The Field Guide to Irish Fairies*, *The Wolfhound Guide to the Shamrock*, *Creatures of Celtic Myth* and *The Truth about the Leprechaun*.

A Haunted Land

IRELAND'S GHOSTS

Bob Curran

THE O'BRIEN PRESS
DUBLIN

First published 2004 by The O'Brien Press Ltd,
20 Victoria Road, Dublin 6, Ireland.
Tel: +353 1 4923333; Fax: +353 1 4922777
E-mail: books@obrien.ie
Website: www.obrien.ie
Reprinted 2005

ISBN: 0-86278-859-5

British Library Cataloguing-in-Publication Data
Curran, Bob
A haunted land : Ireland's ghosts
1.Ghosts - Ireland
I.Title
133.1'09415

2 3 4 5 6 7 8 9 10
05 06 07

Layout and design: The O'Brien Press Ltd
Printing: Nørhaven Paperback A/S

CONTENTS

Introduction

'I believe that there are few speculative Delusions more universally receiv'd than this. That those things we call Spectres, Ghosts and Apparitions are really the departed Souls of those Persons whom they are said to represent.'

'A Moreton' (Daniel Defoe), *Secrets of the Invisible World*

Ghosts have always been with us. As our ancestors gazed out into the gathering prehistoric dusk, perhaps they saw things that were beyond their comprehension and suggestive of their own forebears. It was here probably that the ghost story was born and the tradition has continued down through Classical, Medieval and Victorian times to the present day. And even in these scientific and technological days, phantoms continue to fascinate us, particularly within the Celtic world. Why should this be so? Are there indeed such things as ghosts or is Defoe correct to label them as nothing more than 'Delusions'? Part of the answer may lie in the Celtic tradition and psyche.

The Celts held a very different notion of death than we do today. Nowadays, we view our demise as the end of our interest or involvement in the material, physical world. We do not expect to influence or even to remain in touch with those whom we have left behind or who come after us once we have 'passed away'. This was not the Celtic perspective. Although the Celtic Afterlife was never properly defined – it was usually referred to as some vague and nebulous Otherworld – it remained remarkably close to the sphere of existence of the living. Of course, the Celts held this belief in common with many other ancient cultures, but for them, given their ties of blood and kinship, it held a particular imminence. From their vantage point in the Otherworld, the dead watched their descendants, often with a paternal and friendly eye, and from time to time they intervened in the course of things to benefit those who followed them through the world.

Ghosts were not always terrifying. Although the Victorians did their best to turn them into creatures of menace and fear, most of the early Celtic spectres were benevolent and often returned to the world for a specific purpose. Sometimes it was simply to partake in those things that they'd experienced when alive, for, in the Celtic mind, the world of the dead was simply a kind of pale continuation of the world of the living. There the shades of the dead enjoyed less of the comforts than they had enjoyed in the material world and often yearned to return for short periods to enjoy a pipe, a good, warm fire or a decent meal. And from time to time, they came back to indulge themselves, and those whom they had left behind were required to support them as they did so. The early Brehon Laws – the legal system of the early Celtic world – reflected this, for they decreed that a corpse might own property: a horse, a cow, a suit of clothes and the furniture of his or her bed, and that these could not be sold in satisfaction of debt. The corpse was also entitled to have full enjoyment of these should it decide to return briefly. Tradition also stated that after some time in the cold grave the returning dead required a meal and a glass of spirits, and this was usually provided by the deceased's family. These Celtic revenants, then, seemed to be more corporeal than the drifting phantoms of later times, and they seem to have had hearty appetites as well! They returned from the Afterlife to enjoy the comforts of family life and companionship, and as long as these were provided they were content in their demise. Nor were they particular figures of terror in the community – after all, they were relatives and neighbours and as such were to be welcomed back rather than feared.

There were, however, other reasons which might bring an ancestor back from the Otherworld. From their unseen vantage point, the dead could monitor the affairs of the locality which they had left and maintain a paternal interest in their descendants. So they might come back to intervene in the lives of their children. They could return to warn, to punish, to reward, to advise or to finish work that they'd left uncompleted in life. Thus the Limerick seamstress Grace Connor returned each night from the grave to complete a wedding dress that she'd been paid to stitch before her death, and Daniel McShane came back from the grave to advise his son on the sale of their County Antrim farm. These were functions that they'd probably carried out in life and continued to do so after death.

The Church, of course, found itself in an ambiguous position. It couldn't really condone the idea of ghosts which it dismissed as 'credulous superstition', but it couldn't really deny them either since, by their supposed existence, they provided evidence of the Afterlife. Moreover, there was a Biblical endorsement for their function of issuing warnings and urgings to lead a better life. With regard to sinners and those who turned to evil ways, Luke 16.30 advised: 'If someone from the dead visits them, they will repent!' The dead, it seemed, were actually carrying out Biblical teaching and the Church couldn't wholly denounce them.

Besides, there was another, profitable perspective which the Church might use and which it exploited to its full extent. In doing so it changed the perception of the dead in the Celtic mind. Masses might be said for the dead and Masses meant money for the priests. If families were negligent in the payment of the priest to say such Masses, then the dead might be annoyed (since they were delayed in Purgatory, which appears to be a continuation of the Otherworld, and thus denied their Eternal Reward) and might return to dole out retribution for such neglect. And their vengeance would be awful. And thus the idea of the angry dead was born – phantoms who would terrorise the living and wreak untold horrors upon them. Of course, there had been elements of such things in earlier ghost stories – for instance, tales of the ghosts of malevolent misers or wife-beaters appear in early Roman folklore – but the Christian Church played the perception for all it was worth. Its sole purpose for doing so was to 'encourage' individuals and families to throng into the churches and pay the priests to say Masses for the repose of their dead ancestors. By doing so, people hoped to gain some measure of protection from those who had passed beyond the grave. And, of course, the churches benefited financially from it too.

With the onset of the Age of Enlightenment and the Victorian period, ghosts assumed a rather ambiguous position. On one hand, they were dismissed as pure fantasy, and yet they retained a distinct fascination for many people. Despite the rise of Rationalism and scientific enquiry, there was still what could be described as a thirst for immortality amongst the common people – and the appearance of ghosts served as evidence for the existence of the eternal soul. And yet, there was also an element of danger to these phantoms. In the past they had appeared at all times of the day – midday being a particularly auspicious time to see them – now they appeared only at night-time and in darkened places. It is easy to see why this was so – the gloom and the shadows distort everyday things into monstrous and threatening shapes. Appearances during the night added an air of mystery and menace to the idea of a ghost.

Gradually, spectres became associated in the popular mind with eerie and lonely places – isolated earthen forts, dark clumps of trees, lonely lakes and derelict houses, and the ghost stories and folktales concerning the supernatural usually reflected this. If places looked eerie and were not haunted, ran the wisdom, then they *should* be – and in the later Celtic world, with its rich tradition of tales, there was no shortage of imaginative storytellers to create the associated ghosts.

The histories and character of such places also played a part in these stories. Because of their turbulent pasts, old castles and houses, once occupied by tyrannical noblemen and landlords were often deemed to be haunted. Sometimes, these were the ghosts of the owners themselves, sometimes of their hapless victims. And the undoubtedly fraught history of a place such as Ireland provided many such sites for the tale spinner and for the fertile imagination.

It was from these varying sources – a remembrance of the returning, sometimes hostile, dead, a sense of history and tradition and, just as importantly, a sense of place that the Irish ghost story emerged. This collection, which is based on the folktales and stories that the common people told, deals with all of these aspects. The ghosts which appear in them are of a number of types – child ghosts, dangerous ghosts, the spectres that drift along the corridors of haunted houses, and there are even a couple of what we might call 'celebrity' phantoms. The stories have been divided into two categories – one which reflects the spirits themselves and the missions or impulses that have brought them back from the grave, and the other as ghosts associated with places and specific sites, reflecting both the atmosphere and the sense of history associated with them. The variety of ghosts contained here demonstrates the richness and breadth of Celtic storytelling as well as the influences brought to bear on the tradition, and also the imminence of another world that lies just beyond our everyday vision – a world which can only be vaguely glimpsed with the eye of belief and awe.

So sit back, turn down the lamp, and ignore the wind rising outside, the unaccountable rattling at the back door or the mysterious shadow on the window blind. They're all probably nothing and if you were to look out into the gloom you'd be no better than that ancestor who gazed out into the darkness in fear and trembling. Turn the pages of this book – you are about to enter the realm of the Irish dead where such things might have many different meanings. You are about to enter *The Haunted Land*.

The Spirits of the Dead

The Arny Woman

There is an old saying in some parts of Ireland – 'A man who dies owing money or a woman who leaves a newborn infant will never lie quiet in the grave.' This adage served to remind the living of their main obligations and responsibilities before death. It also forms the central strand of the once widely told tale of the Arny woman from County Fermanagh.

In many country areas, the dead were considered to be extremely possessive – so possessive that they might well return from the grave to claim what they believed was rightfully theirs. Nowhere was this idea of rightful possession more extreme than in the case of a mother and her child. This was a bond which, it was felt, could transcend even death. It was widely believed that mothers who had died during or after childbirth would return to care for their infants. As a child, I remember a woman in our own community in County Down who was supposedly suckled as an infant by her mother's corpse, which had returned from the grave specifically for that purpose.

However, in a more macabre twist, it was also said that other dead mothers missed their children so much that they would appear and carry them back to the tomb if not prevented. One way of preventing this was to place the father's clothes across the foot of the crib – this would ward away 'fairies and the dead' until the child could be formally baptised. If an unbaptised child was taken by the dead, it was lost to the world of the living forever.

This abduction of a newborn by a corpse forms the basis of the story of the Arny woman, but there are a number of other elements in it as well. Certain traits about a living woman might mark her out in the eyes of the local community as 'fairy friendly', and therefore as one who might be malicious after death. These traits included being a 'foreigner' (that is, coming from outside Arny), having red hair, being of a shrewish and spiteful disposition, and having any slight physical deformity.

The role of formal religion in the story of the Arny woman is interesting, for it was not the efforts of a priest that could send her cadaver back to the grave. Rather it was the deployment of Christian symbols supported by an older, more magical wisdom stretching back into the pre-Christian past. This demonstrates a rural Ireland where both Christian and pagan traditions were entwined, where local people paid a kind of devout lip-service to the Church, while also respecting ancient, pagan traditions. This, of course, is not unique to Ireland – the same layering of pagan and Christian traditions can be seen in the Caribbean, in South America, and even in modern cities, such as New Orleans.

Like many rural ghost stories, the tale of the Arny woman is a rich folkloric tapestry with many themes interwoven through it. Once, it was very well known throughout the North, but nowadays it is little more than a fading memory.

About two or three miles beyond Tommy Gilleese's public house at Arny crossroads, a man called Peter Maguire and his wife made their home. Peter was a woodworker and, by all accounts, a quiet and very decent man. His wife, however, was a horse of a different colour.

She was not from the Arny area at all, but had been born away on the other side of Ballinaleck, and nobody in the district knew anything about either her or her family. Nor did they ever find out, for Peter's wife never mentioned her people. A moody and sullen woman, she never made unnecessary conversation or showed any friendliness towards her neighbours. Those that had to have dealings with her found her sharp and uncommunicative, and reported that she was always more ready to issue a curse than a blessing. As a result, no-one in the countryside had a good word to say about her. Not that she seemed to care — Peter's wife kept herself to herself.

Apart from the shortcomings of her personality, there were other factors that made local people uneasy about Peter's wife. Firstly, she had long tresses of red hair framing her narrow, pale face. Red hair, it was said, especially a luxuriant growth like hers, was the sure mark of a witch-woman or of one of the fairy folk. Secondly, one of her legs was a little shorter than the other and she limped. Around Arny, this was a 'fairy mark' and it meant that the woman had close relations with the so-called Good People that lived in secret places in the hills and around the Fermanagh lakes. Thirdly, the people noted that Peter's wife never attended Mass in the church nearby, even though it was only a short walk from her home. All in all, the locals gave her as wide a berth as they could, even though they got on well enough with her husband.

Despite his wife's unpopularity, Peter Maguire appeared happy enough. The woman kept a neat house and appeared docile in public — though this didn't quash rumours that she ruled the roost indoors. There were even stories that she had her husband under some sort of a spell — though no-one ever dared say anything to her face. All the same, local farmers kept their animals well away from her in case she might put the evil eye on them.

For a year or so after their marriage, Peter and his wife were childless. Then, one day, some of the local matrons noticed that Peter's wife's belly was getting big, and shortly after Peter smilingly announced that he was going to be a father. His sullen wife said nothing, nor did her disposition improve with impending motherhood. She was as sharp as ever. Even when neighbour women called to see her and to wish her well, she received them curtly, and made little conversation with them until they left. Although she seemed healthy enough, some of these visitors noticed that the pregnancy was taking its toll. She had never been a robust woman but now she looked even paler and more wasted than usual. This only added fuel to the rumours about her fairy connections, for it's well known that the fairies have great trouble in carrying and delivering their children.

The time approached for the baby to be born. There were many 'handy women' (or midwives) throughout the locality, but the Arny woman didn't call on any of them for help. In fact, she stayed well clear of them, keeping as close to her home as possible. Nobody even knew that the child's birth was imminent, until late one night, Peter Maguire came battering at the door of a neighbour. The baby was coming, he shouted, and his wife was very ill. If she didn't get help, she might not see the night out. Neighbours ran to give aid and between them all, they managed to save the child — a little boy — but they couldn't do the same for Peter's wife. Before morning she was dead. There were many who said privately and out of her husband's hearing that maybe it was no bad thing that she was gone.

There was no funeral in the Arny churchyard for Peter's wife. As Peter struggled to look after his newborn baby, the community took it upon themselves to send her away to be buried in Ballinlaleck, where they'd assumed her family were from. Meanwhile, the baby boy appeared in fine health. Peter brought in a woman during the day to suckle the infant and, at night, the baby slept in a cot at the foot of his father's bed.

One night, a few weeks after his wife's death, Peter was awakened from sleep by a noise. There seemed to be a low scratching sound outside the window of his bedroom. Sitting up in bed, Peter looked out through the uncurtained window into the dark night. Seeing nothing, he shrugged and went to check on his son, sleeping peacefully in his cot. But as Peter climbed back into bed he heard the same low scratching again. He looked out of the window once more — and this time found himself gazing straight into the face of his dead wife.

Her face was extremely pale — much paler than he remembered — and her red hair was matted and listless as it hung down about her shoulders. But it was her lifeless eyes that chilled him to his marrow, for they were looking straight past him and into the room. He followed the dead woman's gaze. Her eyes were fixed on the crib, where their infant son slept.

In that moment, Peter knew why she was there — she'd come back for her baby. He'd heard that mothers sometimes returned from the grave for their children, especially if those children were very young, but he'd never believed such stories, until now. He stared at the dead face of his wife in terror, until just as suddenly as it had appeared, it vanished from the window.

An instant later Peter heard a rattling at the back door. The latch shook but, with relief, Peter remembered the door was bolted. His relief was short lived, for the next sound he heard was the door jamb splintering as the bolt gave way. The door creaked open and Peter knew that the corpse of his wife was in the house.

Leaping into action, Peter placed himself squarely between his bedroom door and the sleeping infant and waited. Instead of trying to come in, however, she placed her face close to a crack in the door itself. He had a glimpse of her hard and glittering eyes in a shaft of moonlight. Then she was gone.

Peter heard scrabbling about in the kitchen, and cupboards opening and shutting. It was as if the corpse were looking for something to eat. Eventually she found a piece of cheese that he'd put away the night before, and he heard her devouring it. Having satisfied her hunger, the corpse then turned and went out through the open door, and disappeared into the blackness.

Behind her in the house, a shocked and shivering Peter Maguire relived what he had seen and imagined what might have happened. He prayed fervently that the corpse of his dead wife had returned to the grave and that this visit might be the end of it.

But the next night, Peter was again wakened by a fumbling at the window of his bedroom and, with a heart that was stopping in fright, he sat up once more. Once more he plainly saw the corpse of his dead wife through the window, trying to open the casement and get into the room. As before, her lifeless eyes were fixed on the infant, who was slumbering in his crib, oblivious to the awful danger. Again she quickly left the window and came round to the back of the cottage, where her husband heard her, rattling at the door. The newly mended bolts and door jamb gave, and the corpse was once more in the kitchen, clattering through the cupboards, looking for something to eat. This time she found some meat that Peter had been saving for the next day's dinner, and she devoured it ravenously. Then, just as suddenly as the previous night, she was gone through the door and out into the dark.

Peter cowered in his own room. He was too terrified to emerge and confront the thing who used to be his wife, though he knew that he could not go on like this. If she came again, he would have to do something.

The next evening, just as it was getting dark, a neighbour man called William Nixon was out for a stroll to Gilleese's pub. To his horror, he saw what he swore was Peter Maguire's dead wife walking the road between the pub and her own house. She was dragging her bad leg after her and keeping close to the hedges. William kept well clear of the ghastly spectre, but was still able to get a good look at her. She had changed in apperance — her matted red hair had grown longer and was now thick with lice and graveyard dirt. Her filthy fingernails had lengthened and seemed much sharper, like the claws of a wild animal. However, he noted she had the same surly attitude that she'd had when alive, and she cast sly glances at him as she went by. William ran to Gilleese's pub and downed several shots of whiskey to try and banish the chill that had settled in his bones. He was still shaking when he finally could tell what he'd seen.

Later that night, back in the Maguire house, Peter had barred the doors with new, stronger bolts and brought his son out of the crib and into his own bed for protection. He'd pulled the bedclothes up over their heads and prayed to be delivered from this awful experience. His prayers must have gone unheard, for soon he heard the now-familiar scratching sound at the window, as the corpse of his wife tried to find a way in.

Peter was holding the child so tight that the baby started to cry. The noise seemed to make the scrabbling at the window even more frantic. Then it stopped. Peter lowered the bed-clothes. Moonlight was shining in through the empty window. From the back of the house came a rattle as the corpse tried the newly strengthened door once more. She found it tightly barred against her and Peter prayed that the new bolts would hold. To his horror, the baby started crying again and, with that, Peter heard the corpse of the child's mother throw herself heavily against the door. With a loud splintering of wood, the bolts gave way and she came crashing into the kitchen. There was a brief tense silence as Peter hushed his child. Then he heard the corpse moving around, looking for a meal.

Peering over the bedclothes, Peter shouted as loud as he could. 'In the Name of God, go back to your grave and leave us in peace!'

It was no good. Not even the mention of the Holy Name made any difference for, although the corpse gave no answer, he heard her moving about the kitchen, gnawing at scraps of food. Then as he held his warm, gently sobbing child to his chest, Peter's heart nearly stopped. He could hear his own bedroom door creaking open. She was in his room!

She was standing close to the foot of the bed, staring at the crib where her son should have been. Peter heard her touch the crib, drawing her filthy hands along the white pillow where her son's head had left its imprint. Peter heard a low growl and she moved back through the door. Then she was gone, back into the kitchen, through the back door and out into the night.

Peter waited a long time before getting up, carrying his son with him. In the kitchen, he found that she'd eaten some beef and a hunk of bread and that she'd spilled some sweet milk. The door had been forced open with a hideous strength – the new bolts, so securely screwed in, had been burst and even the door frame had been completely splintered. Peter Maguire looked at it and trembled. Though she had stolen food, it was really the child that she'd come for, and he knew that this craving would keep drawing her to the house. If he didn't stop her now, there would come a time when she would actually manage to lay hold of the child, and then who knew what would happen? She would wrap the baby in her own filthy shroud and then take him away into the night, back with her to the cold grave near Ballinaleck ... Peter looked at his drowsy infant. He couldn't let this happen. Something had to be done.

Later that day, he went to see the parish priest and told him what had happened. The priest, a country man himself, was frightened by Peter's macabre story. He'd already heard hints and whispers about it from other parishioners. Peter begged him to come up to the house that night and drive away the walking corpse, but the cleric hesitated – he'd a strong fear of ghosts and the walking dead, and certainly didn't want to encounter one himself. No, he finally said, he was afraid he wouldn't be able to come himself. However he'd pray — prayer, he told Peter severely, was the most effective way of sending a cadaver back to its tomb. With that, he gave Peter a crucifix that had been blessed by a Bishop. That, the priest was sure, would keep the dead wife away from the Maguire house. Disappointed, Peter walked sadly away from the priest's house.

As dusk fell, Peter took up a position by the window of his house that looked down the road towards Arny crossroads. That was the direction from which the corpse would come and from here, he could see who or what came up the road and could prepare himself. He threw his own coat across the bottom of the baby's crib to protect the child from evil and harm. Then he sat and waited.

The sun slowly sank behind distant fields until twilight reigned over the countryside. As the last of the daylight failed, Peter saw his dead wife walking very slowly up the road. She was dragging her leg and keeping close to the hedges but her pale face was turned towards the house, and she seemed to be moving with a sense of purpose. Peter gripped his crucifix tighter.

As on the previous nights, the corpse came to the window and looked in, fumbling along the edges of the glass with long, claw-like nails. Peter Maguire thrust the holy cross against it the pane. The corpse drew back, but the icon seemed only to aggravate her, for she then threw herself forward again, her pale face contorted into a mask of utter hate.

Her long fingernails scratched at the glass of the window-pane, filling the whole house with a shrill, grating sound. Her mouth was working, as if showering expletives upon him, though there was no sound. Then she turned quickly and was gone from the window, only to rattle once more at the back door where the bolts had again been replaced. Again she threw herself at the woodwork, and again the door splintered, allowing the corpse to walk into the house.

Peter stayed where he was. He raised the crucifix but kept one hand on his own coat, which lay protectively across the sleeping child in the crib. Pausing for only a moment in the kitchen to quench her thirst on some sweet milk, the corpse came to the bedroom door. There she stopped and stared malevolently at her husband.

'Get back to the grave where you belong!' Peter shouted. 'You'll never have my child! Leave us alone!' The corpse looked at the sleeping child through matted, filthy hair. She reached out her clawed hand as if to touch his smooth face, but then appeared to think better of it. Instead, she wheeled about and left the way she had come in. Peter watched her as she limped slowly down the road dragging her leg. He knew she would return, but he had the beginning of a plan forming in his mind ...

Away near the Bars of Boho, lived a woman called Ellen Mohan. She was widely known as Grey Ellen and fairies were said to frequent her lonely cottage. As dusk settled over the Bars of Boho, Ellen's tiny hovel was often alive with lights and music, as if a throng were merry-making inside. Yet if anyone stopped by her door, there was Grey Ellen on her own, raking the ashes from her hearth or dozing by the drowsy fire. Furthermore, in the evenings, when she came to the doorway of her house, she was seen to bow three times each way to her right and left. People said that she was greeting 'the Gentry' as they call the fairies in that part of County Fermanagh. She was said to be very wise in matters concerning the supernatural and that the fairies had granted her special powers. So it was to Grey Ellen that Peter Maguire went for advice.

Ellen's cottage was in a remote place, well away from the road and over some fields, where the dark trees clustered thickly together. Even in the middle of the day, it was gloomy and Peter's heart was in the back of his throat as he approached it. He'd left his son with his sister and was anxious to be back to protect him before nightfall and the arrival of his dead wife. The day was very overcast and long shadows thronged around Grey Ellen's doorpost. At Peter's approach, crows rose up from the roof ridge, cawing noisily.

Peter knocked and entered to find Ellen sitting on a stool by a low fire, smoking a clay pipe and stirring a black pot. Without even looking up, she motioned him to sit down in a sagging chair facing her.

'Well, what ails you?'

Peter told his tale, and Grey Ellen remained silent for a while. Then she spoke.

'The walking dead, is it?' she asked in a cracked voice. 'An' ye've been to the priest? I'll wager that *he* was of some help t'ye!' she laughed unpleasantly. Grey Ellen had not been anywhere near a church for many years. 'For all its grand book learning, the Church knows nothing about the oul' ways of the countryside!'

Leaning forward on her stool, she gripped Peter's arm with a skinny hand. 'The Church is only any good if it's backed up by the older powers o' the earth an' the land. That's a well known truth.' Her eyes narrowed in the poor light of her dwelling. 'Now tell me — when your dead wife comes to you, does she wear any boots?'

Peter Maguire thought for a moment. 'No', he replied. 'She always comes barefoot, dressed for the grave.'

The old woman made a noise of satisfaction and sucked loudly on her pipe. 'Just so. Tell me, d'ye know why that is?'

Peter thought again but in the end he only shook his head.

'Because of the iron nails in them,' Grey Ellen told him. 'Iron was always a magic metal from the olden times — more powerful than any crucifix that the priest can give ye. Fairies and the walking dead can't stand it anywhere near them. It was a metal that was very important in ancient times and it's important yet.' She laughed without much humour. 'Iron! That's the way to turn away the corpse and to keep her from the cradle until the boy is grown!'

Going to a small box on a ledge beside the narrow window, Grey Ellen took out a handful of iron nails and handed them to Peter. 'Ye've probably ones like these at home but take them for I've no need of them. Put one on a string and put it about the child's neck and keep the others close by you. He must wear the nail like a crucifix until he is confirmed in the church by the bishop himself. If the corpse come into your bedroom, you must throw a handful of the others at her. That'll drive her off.'

Ellen's voice lowered to an urgent hiss. 'This is the *only* means of protection against the dead — it's an old way but it's a sure way. It was used long before there was any Christianity in the country.'

Wonderingly, Peter took the nails that were offered.

'Now go,' said Ellen, 'For I've people comin' t'see me this day an' it's best you're not here when they come.'

In truth, Peter was glad to leave the lonely cottage for the day was dark and there had been odd stirrings in the bushes around the house when he arrived. Who knew who — or what — might be coming to visit Grey Ellen. Casting a nervous glance over his shoulder, Peter stammered his thanks and set out quickly across the fields.

When he got to his sister's house he lifted up his son. The sister watched in astonishment as Peter removed the tiny crucifix the child was wearing, put one of the iron nails on a piece of string and placed it carefully around his son's neck. When Peter told her what Grey Ellen had said, his sister shook her head vehemently. She didn't believe in such things — and, anyway, they smacked of witchcraft. All the same, as as Peter strode down the road towards his house, his infant in his arms, his sister looked after them anxiously and said a silent prayer.

Night had already fallen by the time Peter reached his own front door. The moon had come out, bathing the dark and silent house in a silvery glow. The kitchen door was only partly fixed since the last time the corpse of his wife had broken the bolts and so the back door stood open a little. If the corpse arrived tonight, Peter thought, there'd be nothing at all to stand against her.

Lighting a lamp, he got his son ready for bed. Maybe his wife would stay in her grave tonight, he prayed. He laid the child in his crib and turned to take off his coat. He would throw it across the bottom of the crib as an added protection. As he took off the coat, Peter caught his reflection in a little mirror by the bed. He shrugged — he was looking haggard, older than his years.

In the mirror, Peter could also see the reflection of the rest of the room behind him. Against a wall at the other side of the room was a big, old wardrobe where his wife had kept her clothes. As he gazed at the wardrobe in the looking glass, Peter's blood ran cold, for the wardrobe door was slowly starting to open.

Long, dirty fingernails curled round the edge of the wooden door. As Peter watched in horror, his wife's head followed. Her mouth was open in a snarl, her eyes were full of malice, and long, red hair dropped clods of graveyard earth and scuttling insects onto the stone-flagged bedroom floor. Like a wild panther, she sprang towards the child in the crib, her hands outstretched.

Peter turned to leap in and protect his child, but he wasn't quick enough. The corpse was already over the crib. Suddenly she stopped as if she had been burned. She raised her head and looked straight at Peter, her dead eyes full of astonishment and hate. Grey Ellen had been right — she had seen the iron nail that hung about her child's neck, and its power was turning her back.

Raising herself in front of him, the corpse spat and hissed like a cat. She made frantic, desperate snatching motions in the air over the child's crib that caused Peter to cower in terror. Finally he managed to reach into the pocket of his coat, grab a fistful of nails and fling them at her.

The corpse screamed soundlessly and jumped back in fear and panic. Peter then pulled out the crucifix, even though he knew that it was of limited use.

'Get back t'yer grave, ye witch!' he shouted. 'You're no wife of mine that would harm your own child!'

A single nail had fallen on the edge of the bed. Lifting it, Peter threw it straight at the contorted face of the corpse. It caught her on her waxy, white cheek, and the dead skin sizzled and burned. She drew back with a terrible shriek — the first sound that she'd made since returning from the grave. A massive red welt immediately appeared on her face where the metal had touched her. Scrabbling in panic round the bed-end, the corpse ran out through the bedroom door, across the kitchen and out into the night.

Peter turned to watch his rosy-cheeked son sleeping peacefully. Lifting the coat that had fallen on the floor, he once again laid it gently across the foot of the crib.

That horrific night was many years ago, and it was the last time Peter Maguire was ever to see his dead wife. Although he never forgot his ordeal, the memory of her gradually faded from the community until even her name was lost. Her son grew up; strong and sturdy. He looked after his father in old age, married a local girl and his descendants still live in the locality.

Yet there are still those who quicken their step as they walk from the pub at Arny crossroads past the place where Peter Maguire's house used to stand. All is not quite forgotten — the walking dead cast a long shadow.

The Daylight Wraith

In the annals of Irish ghost lore, the daylight wraith is a curious phenomenon. Traditionally, ghosts are believed to be the spirits of the dead, come back to manifest themselves to the living. They tend to appear during the hours of darkness, in places with which they were associated when alive. Daylight wraiths, on the other hand, are the supernatural appearance of living people. The majority of such wraiths are visions of those who are many miles away at the time – even on the other side of the world. They manifest themselves during the hours of daylight, and in places where the living people couldn't possibly be. They appear to people who know them well, such as their immediate or extended family. On rare occasions, the wraith that appears may even be the image of the viewer him- or herself!

Why does a daylight wraith appear and what function does it fulfill? The usual answer to these questions is that the wraith is a bearer of bad tidings. The sudden appearance of the image of a far-off family member generally indicates to the viewer that that person is either dead or in great need. A wraith that appears as the viewer's own image would be taken as a warning that he or she will be dead within the year. In either of these instances, no violence will be offered, or other harm – apart from shock – sustained.

There are cases, however, when the wraith can turn against those to whom it has appeared. It can throw things and even physically attack those whom it encountered. This would put it in the same class as a poltergeist or 'noisy or violent ghost', another phenomenon that lurks at the edge of supernatural lore. While many ghosts are simply 'seen', poltergeists can often strike, bite and scratch. They also throw stones, break crockery, and upset chairs and furniture in the places where they appear. Some of the so-called daylight wraiths exhibit similar tendencies, which reclassifies them as dangerous ghosts. In these somewhat unusual instances, the wraith can manifest itself both during the day and at night.

Although such spectres have been recorded in Cornwall, the Isle of Man and as far afield as the United States, many of the best and most striking examples of daylight wraiths come from the rural Irish countryside. From the northern Inishowen peninsula of Donegal right down to the Dingle peninsula in Kerry, people recount stories of the wraith. Children have had visions of grandparents living many miles away; mothers have seen sons who are far overseas; and many persons have seen their neighbours who are in some other part of the country. All signify the imminent and usually violent death of the person seen. The most famous of these tales, and perhaps the best documented, comes from the Clogher Valley in County Tyrone and was once widely told all through the North of Ireland. Even today, it lingers on in the memories of many of the old people of the community ...

The old house where it all happened is still there, even though few people mention it much nowadays. It's a desolate and abandoned building, its yard green with grass, its windows broken and slates falling from the roof. Although the land about it is still used, nobody will buy or rent the house itself, even though it's permanently on the market. It stands at the end of a laneway that is so overgrown it is impassable, in the remote district of Cavankirk in the Clogher Valley.

Yet, during the 1890s, this derelict ruin was a stout and prosperous farmhouse, the home of a solid farming family of staunch Presbyterians known as the Wilsons. The Wilsons owned the land around the homestead and further into the Clogher Valley, and were well respected in their local community.

The family consisted of a mother and father, a daughter and two sons. There was very little remarkable about the Wilson children, except that the younger brother, Robert, was wayward, and had a sudden and extremely fierce temper. However, be that as it may, all three of the younger Wilsons led ordinary lives and seemed destined to become farmers themselves.

After both the parents died within a year of each other, the Wilson family continued to live at the homestead. As time went on, the elder two became rather withdrawn, while Robert behaved with a growing recklessness. He argued with the neighbours, almost coming to blows with a couple of them, and he was often seen staggering drunkenly about the country roads. His sister, Lizzie, did her best to reform him but without much success. Robert would calm down, but a few days later he would be as bad as ever. In the end, after landing himself in a couple of serious scrapes involving the local police, Lizzie finally gave up on him. Robert left home and emigrated to Canada.

Life on the home farm continued, pretty much as it had always done. The elder brother, George, continued to run the farm, although now he had to rely on outside help. His sister, meanwhile, ran the house. They seemed happy enough and, if they ever heard from their younger brother in Canada, they never mentioned it. When questioned about him by neighbours, they always gave some vague answer, which suggested that they knew very little about his movements or what he was doing. Mostly they said nothing. That was their way.

One evening, George came into the house looking extremely perplexed. Lizzie asked him what was wrong and he confided in her. In the corner of a field just below the farmhouse, there was a near-ruined, empty stone barn, backed by a high, thick hedge and a ditch. A few years ago, when Robert had been about the farm, this barn had been used for storing tools and so forth, but now it had been cleared out and was completely bare. As he worked away on the other side of the field, George had seen somebody go round a corner and into the barn, disappearing from sight, and from a distance this person had looked very like their brother Robert! Obviously this couldn't be — yet the walk and the way in which the distant figure carried himself were all their younger brother to a 'T'.

Wondering, perhaps, if Robert hadn't returned home unexpectedly, George had run over to the barn. The door was locked and padlocked as usual, and there seemed to be nowhere that the mysterious figure could have gone. Whoever had walked round the corner would have had to walk back up the field to the gate, but nobody had done so. It was all very peculiar, and George suspected that the whole incident had been nothing more than his own imagination. Maybe he'd been thinking momentarily about his brother and thought that he'd seen him in a place with which he'd always been associated. So he'd come back up to the house to take a rest. Lizzie agreed he should lie down for a bit, and there was an end to it.

A few days later in the early morning, just as it was starting to get light, George was raised from sleep by footsteps crunching in the gravel yard below his window. He sat up sleepily and looked out of the window. At first there seemed to be nothing there, but then he thought that he saw a light in the grey morning mist. The light was like that of a lantern moving about in the byre on the other side of the yard. He could tell by the contented lowing of the cattle that they weren't being disturbed by a stranger. But what on earth was Lizzie doing out in the byre at this hour, George wondered? He pulled on his work clothes and rubber boots, and went out to take a look.

As he walked across the yard, George could see through the half-open byre door. He could just make out a shadowy figure moving with the light. It was a man, and from the size, manner and stance, George could have sworn it was his brother Robert!

'Hello?' he called, 'Robert?'

The figure in the byre seemed to half-turn in response to his call. Then suddenly the light went out and the place was plunged into darkness. As George walked closer to the byre in the half-light, he saw to his surprise that the door wasn't half-open at all but firmly locked and bolted.

Was it a dream, George asked himself? Had he been sleep-walking? Wonderingly he went back to the house and got the key for the byre door. He opened the door and went inside. The place was in darkness and the cattle were undisturbed. He stepped back out into the yard. It, too, was empty. George stood there alone as the first streaks of dawn began to colour the sky overhead.

'Hello?' he called again. 'Is there anybody about?'

Only the cry of a late owl from a distant stand of trees answered his question. Shaking his head, he turned and made his way back to the house.

Later that day, the mystery deepened when a neighbour from a nearby farm called at the house. He'd come to do some business with George, but Lizzie brought him into the kitchen for a cup of tea where they waited for her brother to come in from the fields.

'So Robert's home from Canada then?' the neighbour asked, looking all around him. Lizzie's mouth fell open with astonishment and she slowly shook her head.

'Strange,' murmured the man. 'I was sure that I saw him yesterday, walkin' along the bottom of the field below your house — close to the hedge.' He sipped his tea thoughtfully. 'In fact I was so sure that it was him that I called out t'him, his name an' all, but he never answered me an' I thought that he mustn't have heard me.'

Lizzie said nothing, but she was suddenly afraid.

At last George came in and the two transacted whatever business they had, allowing the neighbour man to leave. Alone in the kitchen, Lizzie told George was told about the strange incident. Linked with George's own experiences, the whole affair was becoming very strange indeed, but neither he nor his sister could make any sense out of it.

Each day, the two of them hoped for a letter from Robert to tell them how and where he was. Letters from him had, of course, been very few and far between — he wasn't a good writer — and George and Lizzie hadn't heard anything from him for several months. Lizzie in particular was starting to worry — she had always been close to him. For his part, George continued to work on the farm, seemingly indifferent, although privately he often thought about his younger brother and wondered what he might be doing.

It was obviously preying on his mind. A couple of times as he'd worked about the farmyard, George had been vaguely conscious of a shadow flitting across the yard behind him, just out of the corner of his eye. When he'd turned round, there had been nobody there. On another occasion, George thought that he'd seen the curtains in Robert's old bedroom move, even though there was no-one in the room. Once, he had even seen a hand adjust them, although his sister had been in full view elsewhere. And that wasn't all. A few times, when he was working out in the fields near the house, he'd the distinct impression that somebody was watching him — somebody that he couldn't see — with a malignant and hostile stare.

All these things were relatively trivial — half-dreams and fleeting sensations — but they contributed to an overall feel of unease that was starting to grip the Wilson home. Was George losing his senses, he wondered, or was it the symptom of some other sort of sickness that was affecting him strangely? A couple of times, George thought of going either to see the local doctor or to his local minister, but then thought the better of both. What would he say to both these learned men that wouldn't sound completely mad? It was not, he reasoned, as if he could say that the place was haunted, for didn't ghosts appear at night and hadn't the mysterious figure been seen during the hours of daylight or early in the morning just as the sun was rising? Anyway, as far as he knew, his brother was alive.

Several days later, this belief was strengthened when George and Lizzie received a letter from Robert. He was still as unsettled as ever and was travelling across Canada looking for work. He'd heard that they were taking on men in some of the lumber towns further north and said that he might try his luck there. He was well enough, apart from a slight cold. There was little more to tell — he said that he'd write again soon. George and his sister knew better, but for the time being, their brother's letter put both their minds at rest.

Later the following evening, George was bringing the cattle in from the fields when, a little way ahead of him, he saw the same figure that he'd seen before, walking the edge of a nearby copse of trees. It was certainly late but there was still daylight and he could see the other man clearly. This time he was sure that it was Robert. But how could it be? They'd had a letter from Canada the previous day. Nevertheless, the post was sometimes slow and erratic from such remote corners of the world and it could sometimes take a letter months to come from somewhere like rural Canada. Maybe in the intervening time, George reasoned, Robert had sailed for home and had arrived, unbeknownst to his family, only a day after his message.

'Robert!' George called. 'Robert! Is that you?'

The figure didn't slow or turn around and, not for the first time, George felt the cold prickle of fear on the back of his neck. He called again but, as before, the other simply disappeared amongst the trees of the copse and was lost to view. Leaving the cattle to wander at will, George ran towards the dark tree-stand. The cluster of trees was not very big and there seemed to be no way that anybody could leave it without walking out across the fields. Yet as he approached the copse, George was sure that there was nobody there. There was only darkness under the spreading branches, mixed with flecks of light; between the trees was an unbroken tangle of under-growth, briars and nodding nettles that would bar any wanderer's way. Nobody could have gone in there, even if they'd wanted to.

'Robert?' George shouted again, his voice ragged with fear and confusion. Only the voice of a crow, settling in a field nearby broke the silence. 'Robert? Are you in there?' He tried to enter the copse but undergrowth blocked his way and he had to turn back.

George turned and headed home, puzzled. And yet as he walked away from the spot, the unnerving feeling that some-body was watching him returned.

Back at the farmhouse, the atmosphere was one of lethargy and gloom. While neither Lizzie nor George could say that they were actually ill, both felt off-colour, finding their chores tedious and irksome. George himself put it down to a cold or other virus going about the district but, though she appeared to agree with him, his sister wasn't wholly convinced. A few times, George said that he would go down to see the doctor 'for a tonic' but he never seemed to get round to it. Anyway, he couldn't spare the time. Maybe it was best to let the sickness — if it was a sickness — run its course. After all, it hadn't confined them to bed as yet.

Lizzie, however, was less confident than George. It wasn't just that she was feeling odd. She was also sure that things were being moved around the house if she stepped out — even for a moment. After pegging out clothes, she would return to find a cup in a different place or newspapers moved about. Plates would have been removed from the dresser and sat on the table. Nothing was ever broken or damaged but the situation was inexplicable, and Lizzie was worried about her own mental health. In addition, she couldn't shake the feeling that somebody was watching her — even inside the house — as she went about her daily business.

Both Lizzie and George noticed that the farm animals — especially the dogs — sensed an atmosphere too. They were wandering about the yard in a listless state. The dogs seemed actually unwilling to come into the house, which was odd in itself. George wondered aloud if they had all picked up some sort of strange virus from the livestock.

Sometimes, in the twilit early morning, George would waken, convinced that there was somebody outside his bedroom door. He couldn't actually say that he heard anything but the feeling that there was somebody there was unmistakable. He, too, began to worry. Was he going mad? As he lay in bed, he would try to convince himself that everything would soon be back to normal. 'It's nothing,' he would repeatedly tell himself. 'Just a sickness of some kind. It'll pass.'

About a week after the incident at the copse, George brought the cattle in again and went into the house for his tea.

He was exceptionally tired and he suspected that the illness, whatever it was, was getting a hold on him. His sister had made him a fairly substantial meal, which she'd left heating in the oven of the stove whilst she went out and milked the cattle that he'd just brought in. Taking his meal from the oven, George carried it over to the kitchen table and sat down facing the window overlooking the yard outside.

As George began to eat, the feeling that somebody was behind him began to creep over him again. He'd heard his sister mention this sensation, and on one occasion she'd been convinced that there was somebody standing in the main hall of the house, just beyond the kitchen door. Now, he was sure that somebody was there, staring at him eating — someone with an evil intent. The hostility that washed over him was almost palpable. Then, just as suddenly as the feeling had come, it was gone again, as though something had passed through the hall and out of the house.

George went back to his meal, but as he did so, he thought he saw out of the corner of his eye someone crossing in front of the windowpane. He was sure it wasn't his sister for she would still be in the byre, milking. Once again, he thought of his brother Robert, and then dismissed it immediately. No, it was just his own fancy, as usual.

But as George raised another forkful of food to his mouth, he heard a scream from the other side of the yard. It was his sister! Kicking back his chair, George dashed out of the house and over the yard to the byre.

Lizzie was lying on the ground. As he approached her, she screamed again and cowered away, almost hysterical with terror. It took some time to calm her down so that she could tell him her story. With faltering words, the girl told what had happened and as she spoke, George felt the hairs on the nape of his neck start to rise.

She'd been milking the cows as usual, but they'd seemed restless this evening — in fact, one had almost kicked over a full pail of milk. Then there had been a sudden darkness in the doorway of the byre and, looking up, she hadn't been able to believe her eyes. Her younger brother Robert was standing there looking at her, saying nothing, his face a mask of pure anger. It was as though, she said, a great and terrible hatred were eating him up from inside.

'Robert!' she'd managed to gasp as she struggled to get up from the milking stool. 'How ...? What ...?' She'd assumed that he'd unexpectedly returned from Canada and moved forward to greet him. 'Robert, dear, it's so good to see you ...!'

But instead of rushing into her arms, Robert had given a roar of rage and leapt towards her like a wild animal. The force of it had knocked Lizzie to the ground. Looking up, she'd stared directly into the feral face that loomed over her. The eyes that looked down on her burned with a demonic inner fire, his mouth was drawn back in the very rictus of unholy malice, and his skin was unnaturally livid. Snarling, Robert had placed his hands about her throat and begun to squeeze.

'Robert!' she'd managed to gurgle. 'Are you mad? It's me ...' But Lizzie's words stopped as the pressure about her throat tightened. The weight on her chest seemed to increase and the breath rattled in the back of her mouth. She had been able to feel her senses beginning to slip away ...

Then George had come bursting into the byre and, fighting against the hands on her throat, Lizzie had managed to turn her head in his direction. At the movement, the weight on her body had disappeared. The hands around her throat had melted away like smoke, and the figure of Robert had been replaced with that of George standing over her, gazing down wonderingly.

George helped Lizzie to her feet and led her, gasping and crying, out into the yard. Leaving her leaning against a gatepost, he turned and went back into the byre to search for Robert. But, even as he went, they both knew that he wouldn't find anything, for what had attacked her had not been of this world.

Having made his sister some tea, which she had difficulty swallowing, George took her up to her room for a rest, noting the dark finger-like marks about her throat. He went back to the byre and finished the rest of the milking himself. He was on edge. Every noise about the place startled him and he was glad when the last pail had been filled and he was able to leave. What had the Thing been? It was no wispy phantom, for the bruises on his sister's neck were proof of its solidity and substance. George was dumbfounded. Later, he deliberately walked around the farmhouse and the land, trying to think of an explanation. He saw and heard nothing.

From then on, the feelings of unease about the Wilson farm increased. The dogs became even more skittish about entering the house and would now actually run away from the kitchen doorway whimpering. The unseen activity around the house increased. Loud noises could be heard coming from the kitchen when both Lizzie and George were in other rooms. Sometimes late at night or in the early morning, angry voices could be heard downstairs as George and his sister lay in their respective beds, listening fearfully. Downstairs doors banged and the sounds of crockery smashing floated upstairs — but, upon investigation, everything was as it had been left. The sense of a presence around the house and farm increased. George often turned sharply expecting to see someone behind him, while Lizzie often felt compelled to look into the parlour, sensing that Robert might be sitting there.

Gradually, however, things began to take on a more menacing aspect. One morning, George came down into the kitchen to find that a cupboard had been opened and food lay strewn about the floor. This additional evidence of a malevolent presence sent a chill along George's spine. Whatever was infesting the house meant them harm.

Meanwhile, of course, the glimpses of the distant figure had not ceased. George repeatedly saw the unknown man who looked like his brother walking across a distant field or up the side of a far hill. But George no longer tried to follow. Each time he saw it, the figure now seemed to be walking more quickly than the time before, and was always soon lost to sight. In the farmhouse, the sense of lethargy was replaced by a sense of mounting dread.

Finally, one morning, a letter arrived from Canada. It was not written in Robert's narrow script, but in the broad, awkward hand of a stranger. It was from a man who had shared a room with their brother and with whom he'd become quite friendly, and it carried dreadful news. Out of work for a long time, Robert had turned to drink. One night, at a bar in a northern lumber town, he had become embroiled in a fierce disagreement with some French lumberjacks. The disagreement had degenerated into a serious brawl, a knife had been produced and Robert had been stabbed. He was dead. He had died the same day his sister had been attacked in the byre.

This revelation should perhaps have marked the end of the visitations to the Wilson farm, but it didn't. In fact, the supernatural activity about the place worsened. Formerly, it had been confined to the Wilsons themselves, but now it started to occur when other people were present. Mostly it took the form of noises — voices muttering, the sound of objects being dragged about (although there was no physical evidence of this), sounds of argument in empty rooms. Eventually, neighbours started to avoid the place and even gave George and his sister a pretty wide berth when they chanced to meet them. And there was yet more to come...

One morning, about eleven o'clock, George was out in the yard. Lizzie was very tired and sat down to rest in front of the fire. She'd had a disturbed night — she'd slept fitfully and as dawn began to touch the sky, there'd been noises in the kitchen and in the yard that she'd tried to ignore. As she dozed off in the warm kitchen, she thought she heard a voice speaking softly from somewhere close by — just outside the kitchen door, it seemed.

All at once, something grabbed her from behind. It placed hands about her neck and began to squeeze. It was just like the nightmare experience in the byre only, this time, she couldn't see who her attacker was. Lizzie screamed with all her might and, once again, George came running to the rescue. He had a neighbour man with him, who had also heard the screaming.

As soon as the two men appeared in the doorway, the feeling of great pressure around Lizzie's throat vanished. All was as before. Neither man had seen anything although George later confessed that he had the impression — that was all that it was, just a feeling — that somebody had just stepped out of the room as he stepped in. Despite his solid Presbyterian upbringing, he was now beginning to believe, he told Lizzie, that this 'presence' had been the evil spirit of his brother, Robert.

That evening as he walked round the yard, George himself was suddenly pelted with stones and large pieces of earth, thrown by some unseen agency from one of the barns. The throwing was so ferocious that he had to run for the shelter of the house and shut the door against it. As he ran in, cups and plates started to rattle on the dresser. Both George and Lizzie cowered in the kitchen where they both distinctly heard the voice of Robert calling from the yard ...

George had had enough. He called on the services of the Church. The local Presbyterian minister duly came to the house, but neither heard nor saw anything unusual. The spectre — the daylight wraith — as the clergyman called it, was lying quiet. He said a prayer and read a portion of the Bible before he left. If there were any evil spirits about the place, he said, they would now be routed.

But that evening, as the light began to fail, things were as bad as ever. From the upstairs rooms came sounds like footsteps. Furniture was being pulled backwards and forwards. Objects were being thrown against the walls. There were voices arguing and someone whistling. George and Lizzie were so unsettled that, even when the noises ceased for the night and they went to bed, neither of them could get any sleep.

Once again, over the following days, neighbours insisted that they'd seen a figure in the fields close to the house — a figure that looked identical to their dead brother Robert. These later sightings were all by people other than the Wilsons, and all occurred in broad daylight.

In the end, George and Lizzie could endure it no longer. Though the Wilson family had lived on the land for generations, they sold up, taking a boat for the United States of

America and ending their association with the townland of Cavankirk. With nobody to look after it, the old Wilson place went to rack and ruin. It would be true to say that the locals viewed the ground around it as cursed, for although several neighbouring farmers bought, leased and sold it, the property never really prospered and none of them made money from it. Its reputation for being haunted never left it. There were those around the countryside who said that, even though the main dwelling house was falling down, they'd seen a figure standing in the overgrown, weed-choked yard, or coming and going from the locked, dilapidated barns.

And that's the way it remains today. The farmhouse is now a dreary ruin and the farmyard has long disappeared under a sea of briars, nettles and tall grasses. A few of the old out-houses can still be seen, though they are as desolate as the ruined house. The name of the once-respectable Wilson family is now all but forgotten.

But the story lingers in the minds of the older people in the district. Despite the march of progress, the area is still remote and the old beliefs are alive and well. As the sky begins to lower above the ruined farm and the day draws to a close across Cavankirk, it isn't hard to imagine that there are supernatural beings moving along the roadways, across the fields or in the shadows of hedges — otherworldly creatures, such as Robert Wilson's daylight wraith.

The Legend of
Frank McKenna

From the Sperrin Mountains of County Tyrone, the tale of Frank McKenna combines two fundamental strands of Irish ghost lore. Firstly, it contains a strong moral element by demonstrating how a spectre can be trapped on Earth through religious negligence. Secondly, McKenna's phantom becomes a prophesying 'celebrity' ghost, consulted by local people on all manner of subjects.

Once again, this story illustrates the ambivalence of the Church towards ghosts. The ghost is used by the local priest as a warning to those who abandon or neglect their religious duties. Later, however, the 'false spirit' is denounced for leading local people astray with its predictions. The ghost in this case is not the solid, almost corporeal phantom of most ancient Celtic lore. Rather it takes on the insubstantial, ethereal form of Anglicised Victorian ghost lore. This version may be a product of the time and location involved, for in the late nineteenth and early twentieth centuries there was a strong Anglo-Saxon element all across the North, even in remote places, such as the Sperrins.

The tale was once very widely known all across the North — there are even some very old people today who can point out places where Frank McKenna's ghost appeared. The actual location of Frank McKenna's farm, however, is problematical. Along the Tyrone–Monaghan border, there are a number of McKenna families who live in the area where Frank's phantom is said to have appeared. However, given the circumstances of the legend, none of these families have claimed association with the ghost. Few people, even now, wish to discuss a 'false spirit' with strangers — yet the ghost of Frank McKenna still haunts the lonely roads and trails that wind through the mountains, casting his spectral shadow into rural folklore ...

At the very end of the nineteenth century, near the Tyrone–Monaghan border, there lived a young man by the name of Frank McKenna. Frank's family were decent people who worked hard, farming the land that swept up from the Monaghan border into the foothills of the Sperrins. However, as the youngest of the family and the only boy, Frank himself was a rather cocky and headstrong individual. He would take no advice and little bidding from his parents on even the smallest matter. As the only son, he was sure of inheriting his father's prosperous farm in due course, and this caused him to affect the airs and graces of a 'country gentleman'.

In spite of these flaws, Frank was well liked throughout the countryside, for he had a pleasant temperament and was excellent company. There wasn't a pub or drinking house that didn't welcome his ready wit and easy charm — though it was acknowledged that, if he were crossed, he had a quick temper.

Frank's passion was hare-coursing, a favorite regional pastime. Each weekend, Frank and the young men of the parish would take themselves off to the mountains with packs of dogs. There they would have great sport chasing hares and rabbits all across the country — the winner was the man whose dogs caught the largest hare. Frank McKenna, always fiercely competitive, never missed a hunt and often returned in triumph. Always conceited, he positively revelled in his reputation as the best hare-courser in the district.

Yet, despite this apparently blessed life, there were one or two old people in the area — those widely reported to be cursed with visions — who said there was a dark cloud hanging over the shoulders of Frank McKenna like a winding sheet, and that he might not be long for this world. For his part, Frank, so young, so arrogant and so full of life, found it easy to ignore these doomy predictions.

One Sunday morning near Christmas, when both the sun and the air were sharp and clear and there was a sprinkling of snow on the distant Sperrins, Frank McKenna rose and put on his heavy walking brogues. His father, who'd risen before him and was seated at the kitchen table, eyed him suspiciously.

'Why're you putting those on?' he asked. 'Surely you're putting on your good boots and coming to Mass with the rest of the family?' Frank looked back at him a little askance.

'Indeed I'm not,' he said in a surly voice. 'It's a fine, crisp day and the hares'll be risin' in the mountains. There's some of us taking the dogs an' goin' up there for a bit of a hunt. There'll always be a Mass down in the chapel but there'll be very few days like today.' With this, Frank laughed gaily. 'The priest can wait on us another week!'

Frank's father looked at him in angry surprise, not only by such insolence but also by his blasphemy.

'You'll come to Mass with us this morning!' he thundered angrily. 'No son of mine'll neglect his religious duties!'

The old man's insistence seemed to amuse Frank, who just smiled at this and shook his head.

'Religious duties can be done at any time, Father,' he said smugly. 'I'm bound for the mountains and for a day of sport with the hares.'

Frank's father's frown deepened. He knew how obstinate his son was, and that he would not be turned when in that frame of mind.

'Then you'll go without my blessing,' he snapped. 'It's an impious act you're committing this day!'

At that any remaining vestiges of duty in Frank vanished. He would definitely not go to Mass now — maybe he would never go again!

'I'm away to the mountains,' he announced. 'The hares'll

be starting up with the sun and there'll be a grand day's hunting today. We'll have rare oul' sport. Goodbye, Father!' he
called as he walked across the kitchen to the back door.

'My blackest curse on you!' spat Frank's father from the
kitchen table. 'No good can come from neglecting your religion. God Himself will punish you for your impudence!'

The old man's threats were lost on Frank McKenna for his
temper was roused and he'd made up his mind. Lifting his
cock-stick which stood against the kitchen wall, he threw
open the door and went out into the bright morning, whistling indifferently to himself.

'Ah, Frank!' his father pleaded one last time, following
him out. 'Think again! You should be paying attention to
your eternal soul rather than some sport in the mountains.'

But Frank McKenna did not even reply, and strode non-
chalantly along the lane that led down to the road.

'Well, then, the Devil take you for your blasphemy!' the old
man shouted after him, hot with anger. 'No son of mine is
welcome in this house if he turns his back on his religion!
May you never come home again!'

Frank's whistling drowned out the old man's ominous
words. At the sound, his dog came bounding after him and
stayed close to him as he walked.

By the time Frank got to the village crossroads, a crowd of
young men and their dogs had gathered. The day was sharp
and bright and promised great sport, and there was plenty of
teasing and laughing as the lads set out for the Sperrin

Mountains with their hounds at their heels. As they wound their way up into the foothills, hares and rabbits started up in front of them. Soon the dogs were chasing through the humps and hillocks all around, baying loudly as they went.

The young men all knew the mountains well — and knew that they could be dangerous as well as beautiful. There were a number of deep hollows in which lay treacherous bogs, and there were gullies in which a hunter and his animals could be lost forever. In the mountains, mist could descend in an instant, blotting out all the familiar tracks and landmarks and leading travellers far from the safe pathways.

These concerns, however, were not foremost in the minds of the crowd as they climbed higher and higher among the slopes. They chased and caught several hares and the *craic* was great.

However, Frank wasn't having a good day. He only caught a couple of hares, while the bags of the others were growing bulkier by the minute.

'Well, Frank,' teased his cousin Michael Trainor, 'It looks like you're going to lose your grand name of being the best hare-courser in the district!' But Frank, as was his manner, only shrugged his shoulders and gave a knowing wink.

'The sport's not finished by a long way, lads!' he said. 'And there's plenty of hares still out there in the hills. I'll bag a few of them yet before I go home!'

Suddenly one of the crowd shouted and pointed. Sitting on the top of a nearby rise was a large, brown buck hare, almost as big as a small dog. No-one had ever seen a hare as enormous as this. It was watching the hunters below with an almost human eye and showed no fear at all. Though they turned in its direction, it never moved.

'What did I tell you?' Frank McKenna told his cousin. 'That's the one for me! That's the one that I've been waitin' on.' And whistling up his dog, he sent it bounding after the brown hare.

The creature sprang into action and was gone from the rise, leaping between rocky outcroppings and stones at a terrific speed straight towards the highest peaks of the mountains. Frank's dog followed and Frank himself soon broke into a run over the uneven ground in pursuit of his prey. Although he was agile and quick on his feet, the ground was dangerous and, as he drew further away from them, his companions shouted after him to be careful.

As Frank scrambled further and further up the slope, Michael Trainor grew more anxious. 'Leave the hare and come back down, Frank!' he shouted. 'It's not worth getting hurt or lost up there!'

But Frank McKenna simply kept on going. Soon the others became restless and the sport began to sour for them.

'We're going back down home now, Frank!' somebody shouted.

Frank didn't seem to hear. The heather and briars tore at his trousers and legs, drawing blood. He didn't feel it, for the strange brown hare kept rising up suddenly in front of him, and he and the dog kept plunging after it. Sometimes it was so close that Frank could nearly touch it. Other times, it rose on a hillock or rock way off in the distance. Soon Frank was deep into the Sperrins, climbing up shallow glens and scrambling through small streams where he'd never been before.

Further down the mountain, somebody grabbed Michael Trainor's arm. 'Look up there!'

A greyish mist was rapidly descending from the mountains above them. Frank, although he was a good way up, didn't seem to have seen it.

'Frank!' Michael cupped his hands to his mouth. 'Frank! For God's sake, turn back, man!'

It was no use. As the mist came sweeping down, the hare, Frank McKenna and his dog all vanished into it. Then, just as suddenly, the mist halted and came no further.

The young men drew further back down the slope behind them. Although they were full of bravado when hare-coursing, they were all local men and deeply super- stitious, and this grey fog had an uncanny feel about it. They decided as one to start for their homes — if Frank McKenna wanted to go further up the mountain than any of them had ever been, it was his own business and he could make his own way home. Nevertheless, they came down out of the mountains in silence, for their mood had changed. Each was hoping that Frank would follow them down, and that he would be seen drinking in a pub before the end of the day.

Frank did not return. For two days nothing was heard of him. His distraught family watched and waited for his familiar figure to stride up the lane, holding his cock-stick under his arm like a country squire, and whistling for his hound. But no such figure arrived home. There were stories about him as there often are in such situations. Some said that he'd staged the whole affair himself as some sort of joke and that he was alive and laughing at them all. Sightings of him abounded — he'd been seen crossing the street in Emyvale, he'd been seen drinking in a pub in Clones, he'd taken up with a woman in Monaghan town, he'd been seen at the door of a house in Fivemiletown. But all the stories were second- or third-hand, and nobody was ever truly sure.

Then, on the evening of the second day, Frank's bedraggled dog returned alone. Its coat was wild and torn by brambles and it seemed to have a strange manner about it. When Frank's father approached it, the animal cowered away and bared its teeth — nobody could understand, for the dog had always been such a friendly animal. More worrying was the fact that everyone knew that Frank and his dog were inseparable — everywhere he went, his hound followed him. It was almost unthinkable that it should come home without him. This only confirmed everybody's worst fears: something must have happened to Frank up there on the lonely mountainside.

A search party was put together the following morning. It hunted across the uplands all day without finding any sign of him. When the day darkened, the search party returned home, but set out bright and early again the following day; traversing gorse-grown slopes and tiny rivers, tracing trails that hadn't seen a human foot for years.

At the end of the fourth day, they found Frank.

He was dead, of course, lying on the edge of a bog, high up among the Sperrin peaks. He looked as if he'd fallen from sheer exhaustion, and the cold of the high mountain nights had probably finished him off. His cock-stick lay, broken in two, on a rock, a little way from the body. Near the place where he'd died were old standing stones and earthworks from very ancient times, and the sun cast strange shadows across them on the neighbouring slopes. On finding him, the men of the search party crossed themselves, out of respect for his soul and out of fear for themselves. With heavy hearts, they carried the body down from the mountain and back to his grieving family.

The day of Frank McKenna's funeral was grey and sombre, but there was a huge turnout to see him being laid to rest. As the band of mourners made their way from the house to the local cemetery, one old man pointed up to a rise close to the road. There, watching the funeral pass by was an enormous brown hare, identical to the one that Frank had followed up the mountain to his death. Angrily, one of the youths lifted a stone from the roadside and threw it at the animal. The hare bounded away but not before the missile had caught it on its right side. There was a loud sound like a stick striking a hollow drum and then the creature was gone. The mourners muttered amongst themselves for there was something supernatural about the hare. All about them, the day seemed to darken and they quickened their steps towards the churchyard and holy ground. Not for the first time, Frank's heartbroken father bitterly repented of the curse that he'd levelled at his son the last time he saw him alive.

Months went by and gradually the name of Frank McKenna faded from the memories of all but his grieving family. His father was now a broken man and the whole farm seemed to reflect the waste of Frank's lost young life. But in the wider community, life returned to normal — and might have continued this way had it not been for an extraordinary occurrence.

In a remote mountain area, near to where Frank's body had been found, a shepherd named Daley lived in a ramshackle two-room cabin. His wife had been dead for some years and he lived with his daughter, Rose — a girl of fifteen or sixteen — tending sheep that wandered about the mountain slopes. He was generally said to be a decent man, though sometimes distant and secretive in his ways. Rose was a dreamy, wistful creature who was given to wandering the hills and hidden hollows around her cabin home.

One night, Rose awoke to find the image of Frank McKenna standing at the foot of her bed. She had heard all about the strange death, and had even known him by sight in life, but now he looked different. He seemed older, his sad face had lost its youthful cockiness and had an unhealthy pallor about it. He was dressed in the clothes in which he'd died — a heavy jacket and trousers and his walking brogues. Under one arm was his unbroken cock-stick.

Frank was gazing down at Rose with a doleful expression. Worse still, the girl could see through his body to the wall of her own bedroom. She could clearly see the holy picture that her father had pinned to the plaster and the edge of the little dresser that was the only furniture in her bare room.

'Who are you?' she cried out, although she already knew the answer. 'What d'you want here?'

'I'm Frank McKenna,' whispered the ghost. 'I died in a mountain bog many months ago. I chose pleasure in the mountains over duty in the church and now I'm condemned to wander the same mountains forever!'

The spirit spoke to her in such a melancholy tone that the girl lost a little of her terror. 'What d'you want from me?' she asked. McKenna's ghost paused for a moment.

'Because of my indifferent ways,' he answered mournfully. 'I'm unable to enter either Heaven or Hell but doomed to walk the world for Eternity. Go and see my father and tell him to ask the parish priest, Father Purcell, to say a Mass for the repose of my soul. He'll find money to pay the priest behind the old clock in my room. And tell my friends and them that knew me not to neglect their religion or they too will suffer my fate!'

And with that the ghost was gone, leaving only the moonlight streaming in through the cabin's uncurtained window. Disturbed by what she had seen, Rose went and roused her father who was snoring in the next room. He'd heard nothing. Together they sat and puzzled it over. By morning both of them concluded that it had been nothing more than a bad dream and that they should forget about it.

The next night, however, Rose awoke again to find the ghost of Frank McKenna standing at the bottom of her bed.

'Go and speak to my father!' he urged her. 'The longer you delay, the harder it will be to save my soul!'

Rose considered for a moment. 'But how do I know that you're really a spirit — and the spirit of Frank McKenna to boot?' she asked. 'For all I know you might be some evil ghost come to lead me into temptation and wickedness. Or you might merely be a bad dream resulting from the bit of cheese I ate before bedtime.'

McKenna's ghost stared at her mournfully, and then spoke.

'All things, no matter how small, are known to those who are dead,' he whispered. 'Things that are hidden from the living. Tomorrow morning a black crow will come and peck three times at your window. When this happens, you will know that this is not a dream. Now go to my father and have the Mass said. I crave some peace!'

When Rose looked again, the ghost was gone.

The poor spirit had sounded so distraught that Rose fell asleep wanting to believe in him. The following morning, a black crow did indeed come to her window and peck three times, just as McKenna's ghost had predicted. For Rose, that settled the matter and she wasted no more time. She went straight down to McKenna's farm and asked his father to do as the spirit had instructed.

At first, the old man wouldn't believe her — his son lay buried in the holy churchyard clay, he insisted, and was not wandering about on some lonely mountain side appearing to young, dreamy girls in the middle of the night. But Rose urged the old man to look behind the clock in Frank's room for the money to pay the priest. To the father's astonishment, the money was there. He hadn't known about it, so how had the girl known? He took the money as instructed and went to Father Purcell. The following day, a Sunday, Mass was duly said for the repose of Frank McKenna's soul.

Father Purcell used the occasion to remind his congregation of their religious duties and obligations.

'Never neglect a holy day,' he thundered from the pulpit, 'Else you too may finish up wandering over the mountains as a ghost. Take heed of the fate of Frank McKenna. And if you don't believe me, go up to that lonely cottage and hear of the earth-bound spirit for yourselves — proof of the awful judgment of God on those who are neglectful of their religious obligations.'

It was a stern warning. Several took the priest at his word and went up to Daley's remote hut, high in the Sperrins. They wanted to talk to Rose Daley and hear about how the ghost had appeared and warned her of her obligations. But they also wanted to hear again about how McKenna's ghost had claimed the gift of prophecy. They wanted McKenna's ghost to answer questions about what lay in store in the future.

When McKenna's ghost appeared that night, he was taken aback by the number of people who had crowded into the hut. Some of the braver souls called on the spirit to prophesy and, after a little persuasion, he obliged. Much to the wonder of everyone present, he revealed certain things that would occur in the course of the coming month and stated that these prophesies were certain to happen. He also disclosed a number of facts about certain families living in the area, to the amusement and wonder of his audience.

Word went round the parish and soon a fair pilgrimage of people were making their way up into the remote Sperrins and to Daley's door. The small cabin was always full. Each night, McKenna's ghost would appear at a certain hour and with each appearance, he seemed more and more like the old Frank McKenna that they had known. Loving all the attention, he became witty and humourous. He told stories and jokes and sang songs. At the end of each evening and on a payment being submitted to Daley himself, McKenna's ghost would reveal the immediate futures of those present and disclose secrets that scandalised the countryside. Poteen was often produced at these gatherings, which went on until cockcrow. In fact, Daley's cabin became something of a shebeen, frequented by all sorts of people.

As his audience grew, the spirit's predictions and disclosures became more outrageous and salacious, and his manner became more bawdy and boisterous — just as Frank McKenna's had been when he was alive. No-one was safe from his all-knowing eye, not even the local clergy, about whom he revealed a number of hilarious secrets.

Eventually, news of these goings-on reached the ears of Father Purcell and Frank McKenna's family, all of whom were outraged. Having initially encouraged people to go and take warning from the spirit, the priest now issued another strong warning from the pulpit.

'The so-called ghost of Frank McKenna is a false spirit,' he announced. 'And one that has come to lead God's people into great wickedness! These nightly gatherings at Daley's must stop and no heed must be paid to the words spouted by the false spirit! This is the instruction of your priest!'

On hearing this from the people gathered at Daley's the following night, McKenna's ghost simply laughed.

'Let him instruct all that he likes,' he told those gathered in Daley's cabin. 'I can tell you things about his background if I've a mind to!'

So the gatherings continued. By now, the prophecies of McKenna's ghost had become such a famous wonder that people started coming from miles around for a consultation. Farmers unsure about stock or land, those wanting advice on a business venture, young men and women considering marriage — all made their way into the Sperrins to consult with

Frank McKenna's ghost and to catch a glimpse of their future. And the ghost advised them all for the small fee, which was paid directly to Daley.

In utter frustration, Father Purcell, backed by Frank's family, took the matter to the Bishop. The Church authorities viewed it extremely seriously and a letter was read out in every pulpit between Dungannon and Monaghan Town. The letter expressly forbade anyone from consorting or consulting with false spirits on pain of a public shaming — or perhaps even excommunication. At this last threat, congregations finally took heed, and soon the flow of people to Daley's cabin had fallen to a mere trickle. McKenna's ghost appeared more and more rarely until, eventually, he disappeared altogether. Within a year, life in the mountains had returned to normal, and the Daleys' hut became as quiet as before.

Soon the story of Frank McKenna's ghost had become no more than a local folktale. Some people, including Father Purcell, said that it had all been no more than a trick, performed by Daley and his daughter, to get money from gullible souls. Others said that it had really been a demon that had set out to confuse God's children and that it had been driven away by the Church.

Daley and his daughter moved to a different county and their cabin fell to rack and ruin. The mountain wind came and went through the sagging doorway and glassless windows and soon even the mud walls fell in on themselves. Today there is no trace of it or where it stood and only a few people across the mountains even vaguely remember Frank McKenna's ghost. Even so, some local people still avoid the area where the cabin is thought to have stood. Most people simply say that it's an 'unlucky' spot.

One old man led me up to the throat of the lonely glen where Daley's house was believed to have stood, although he wouldn't go down into it. It was getting towards evening, and I could tell that he was a bit nervous even of being there.

'They say that even on the warmest day, the air's very cold down in that place,' he told me, gesturing down into the hollow in front of us. As we sheltered from the sharp mountain wind behind a great stone, the old man told me the legend of Frank McKenna.

'He was a very famous ghost in his day,' he said, 'And it fairly put the wind up the Church, so it did!' He laughed and spat into a nearby pond. 'There are still some old people who say that they've seen his spirit wandering about down there among the stones and rocks, even yet. They say yon glen's still badly haunted.'

The wind sighed amongst the great outcroppings of stone a little further up the slope behind us — a long, eerie, drawn-out sound, like a soul in torment. Quite suddenly, I didn't want to be there. Looking down into the gloomy valley under a failing sun, I felt that perhaps the spirit of Frank McKenna wasn't as far away as I would like.

The Radiant Boy

Child-ghosts have been a common enough phenomenon in Irish folklore and sightings of them are to be found all across the country. The ghost of a small boy, for example, is said to haunt the gate-lodge at Rathfarnham Castle at the foot of the Dublin Mountains. The woeful spectre is said to have been connected with the horrific murder of a child within the walls of the tiny house, though the exact circumstances of the slaying have been long forgotten. Even so, the ghost is still seen, sometimes close to the gate-lodge door, sometimes peering out of one of the windows, by visitors to the castle and by passers-by alike.

Similarly, the phantom of a little girl is said to haunt the corridors and rooms in the famous Shelbourne Hotel, near Stephen's Green, Dublin. The Shelbourne, a respectable old edifice, has a long history, which may account for the great variety and frequency of ghostly appearances. In fact, at one time, the number of sightings became so great that, in order to protect its reputation, the hotel called in a medium who made contact with some of the ghosts – including the ghost of the little girl. It was discovered that her name was Mary Masters and that she'd died at the Shelbourne, but little more is known – including who she was or how she died.

I have a personal experience of a child-ghost that has remained in my memory down the years. Many years ago, when living in County Down, I was working with a neighbour, delivering some items to another farm in a remote rural district. We arrived at the farm on a particularly bleak winter's day, filled with pelting rain mixed with snow. It was late evening and the woman of the house had the lamps lit and the tea ready for us when we arrived.

As we crossed the yard to the house, my companion saw a small boy standing in the doorway of an outhouse watching us. He assumed the lad to be a child of the house and, anxious to get out of the rain, he didn't mention him until we were inside. As we sat in the warm kitchen, with the supper in front of us and the family gathered round, he expressed some surprise.

'Are you not going to bring that wee boy in and give him something to eat with us?' he asked. 'He looks very cold!'

The woman of the house drew back with a start.

'Where did you see him?' she asked. My friend pointed through the kitchen window, over towards the door of the outhouse that was now empty.

'He was there a minute ago, as plain as day,' the man answered, sensing that something was wrong. 'A wee boy about six or seven years old, very thin and pale-looking. Who is he?'

'Ah! That poor lad sometimes comes about this time of the evening,' she answered. 'And always about this time of the year, though not everybody can see him.'

The child, she explained, was the ghost of a boy who'd lived at the farm years before. One winter's night he'd gone out into the yard, fallen into an old slurry-pit (a deep pit full of farmyard manure and waste) and drowned. Heartbroken, the family sold up and moved to another part of Ireland.

'But even though they're long gone,' the woman went on, 'And the place is now ours, he still comes back here sometimes. I've never seen him myself but there's plenty that have. He just stands about the yard, late in the evening and watches what's going on, just like any other wee boy. Sure there's no harm in him. No harm in him at all.'

As we drove away from the farm, my friend looked out of the car. He could clearly see the boy, he said, standing by the corner of a barn in the shadow of a big turf-stack, watching us go. I, myself, saw nothing.

Whilst this particular ghost might well have been mistaken for a living child, other child phantoms had a distinct supernatural appearance. These are 'radiant children' – eerie child phantoms that are surrounded by a flickering brilliance. One example is the glowing ghost of a little girl, who visits a certain house in Killyleagh, County Down, every seven years. She is believed to have been murdered there by her mother.

These radiant phantoms sometimes have a more sinister aspect than the little boy in the farmyard. They are warning ghosts, and to glimpse them means that the viewer may not have long to live. They may not be associated with any particular location but, like the banshee, may follow those whom they have 'marked' wherever they go – becoming a kind of peripatetic phantom. The most famous of these, recounted by the celebrated Victorian writer, Catherine Crowe, comes from the North of Ireland, and hinted at severe consequences for a certain well-known figure …

It was the mid-1700s. Captain Robert Stewart, an officer in the British Army stationed in the developing port of Belfast, was enjoying his day's hunt further north in County Derry. The day had started off bright and beautiful and Stewart, a keen horseman, soon put some distance between himself and the rest of the hunt, pursuing game into a low range of hills.

Then, without warning, the weather turned ugly. The captain found himself riding into a fierce rainstorm. The further he rode, the worse the downpour became until, desperate, he realised he had to find shelter. Through the rainy murk, he saw the faint glimmer of a light. Turning his horse in its direction, he rode towards it, rain dripping from his face and clothes.

There was an ancient mansion emerging from the gloom. The light that the captain had seen came from one of its windows and, as he drew closer, he saw brightly lit windows, and heard sounds of merriment and laughter from within. In the forecourt of the mansion, Captain Stewart called for assistance and several menservants came running to attend him. There was a party in progress, they said, and the place was filled with guests. Nonetheless, the Captain would be made very welcome.

Sure enough, the master and mistress of the house were kindness itself. They had heard of Captain Stewart and of his family, and quickly invited him to join in the party. It was a jolly affair with plenty to eat and drink, and Stewart's host dropped strong hints that the captain might stay for a few days and join the other guests for some shooting and fishing. Although tempted, Captain Stewart refused saying that he'd urgent business back in Belfast, but that he was glad of the invitation and would certainly take it up at some future date.

At last, an agreeable evening drew to a close, and many of the guests departed for bed. Outside, the storm showed no sign of abating, with the wind and the rain lashing harder than ever against the sturdy walls of the old house. Stewart's host prevailed on him to stay the night.

'Believe me, sir,' said the man, 'I wouldn't turn out a dog on a night like this! Stay until morning and have breakfast as our guest. By then the storm should have blown itself out.' He gestured to a servant who stood nearby. 'Hamilton here will show you to a room.'

Stewart considered. He certainly wanted to get back to Belfast but the storm was still at its height and it was not a night to be travelling. Besides, it would be most discourteous to refuse such a kind offer. Gratefully, he accepted the other's hospitality.

The old manservant led the young officer along a series of twisting corridors and up narrow staircases to a large room at the very back of the ancient house. The chamber looked as though it had once been a grand guest-room, but had obviously not been used as such for some time. It was almost bare of furniture apart from a divan bed in one corner, several chests, a couple of chairs and an old wardrobe. However, a maid had lit a large peat fire in the grate, which threw out a comforting heat and a sweet smell. The servants had prepared the bed and had covered it with cloaks and coats for warmth. These would be much needed, thought Stewart — despite the fire, the room seemed distinctly chilly.

After the old manservant had said goodnight, given him a candle and left, Stewart yawned. It was not the luxury he would have hoped for, but the room was cosy enough and he was exhausted after a long day's hunting. Wearily, he lay down and soon sank into a fitful sleep. Outside the wind howled dismally, sucking the flames of the fire up the chimney.

Captain Stewart awoke to a soft, insistent sound coming from the darkness around him — the sound of a child crying quietly. Blearily, he rose from his makeshift bed. Raising the candle, he looked around. He could see nothing.

After checking the room again, the sounds eventually seemed to fade away.

'It must be a trick of the wind,' thought Stewart. He returned to his bed and, extinguishing his candle, dozed off once more ...

The captain had not been asleep long when he was once again disturbed. This time, it was not the eerie, far-away sounds that roused him but a fierce and vivid grey light flooding the room. At first, the captain thought that the house was on fire, and jerked fully awake. Then he looked across the room and gasped in astonishment at what he saw.

Crouched in the far corner, to the left of the antique wardrobe, was a naked boy, his head turned towards the oak-panelled wall. The child was crying bitterly, his bare shoulders rising and falling with each heartbroken sob. To Captain Stewart, it seemed as if the distressing sounds came from a long way away, from some distant, echoey place. The figure seemed so sad and pathetic that the young officer's heart went out to him. Rising from his bed once again, Stewart crossed the room to the crying child.

'What is it?' he asked. 'Why do you weep so?'

The figure made no reply, but continued to cry in a truly pitiful manner. Stewart stretched out his hand to touch the naked shoulder. As he did so, the boy suddenly vanished and the room was plunged into darkness, the only light being the dying flicker of the fire in the grate. The storm rattled at the shutters.

Captain Stewart suspected that some of the other party guests were playing a trick on him. They must, he reasoned, be hiding somewhere close by, having a laugh at his expense — it was all probably a monstrous prank to terrorise him. Fuming at the idea, he returned to bed and fell again into a shallow sleep.

The next morning, Stewart felt annoyed and tired after his disturbed night. He went straight to his host and confronted him over the breakfast table. He complained that he'd been the victim of some practical joke during the night and that such behaviour was unworthy of a host towards a stranger and a guest in the house.

The master of the house, although he was somewhat taken aback by the story, did not consider it beyond the realms of possibility that some of the younger men might have engaged in a jape. In front of the assembled company, he appealed for them to declare themselves and make an apology to his offended guest. The young men present, however, all declared emphatically that no such joke had taken place. Those not present at breakfast were summoned, and also produced similar sincere denials. The whole thing was a mystery.

Suddenly a thought occurred to Stewart's host. Summoning the old manservant, he asked, 'Hamilton, what room did you put the Captain in last night?'

The elderly man looked sheepish. Moving from foot to foot, he replied in an apologetic tone. 'Well, Sir, the house was very full as you know — gentlemen were lying four in every room — so I had a fire and a bed made up for him in … one of the back rooms that's never used.'

A sudden pallor crept across his master's face and he took a step back.

'You don't mean the Boy's Room?' he asked, his voice little more than a whisper.

'Yes, Sir,' the old servant answered softly. 'I didn't think that he'd actually see anything. It's just an old story, isn't it? I mean, there's nothing actually there …?'

His master didn't answer, though the silence spoke volumes.

'You were very wrong to do so, Hamilton,' he said at length. 'You know that I've expressly forbidden anybody to occupy that room and that I've even taken most of the furniture out of it to prevent anybody from so doing. Make sure that it's now closed up and that nobody can enter it again!'

The old man turned to do his master's bidding, whilst Captain Stewart looked on with astonishment.

'You must forgive Hamilton, Captain,' his host said. 'He's always anxious to please and in his eagerness he sometimes forgets the traditions that have blighted this family for many years — from a time before he himself was a young boy.'

Captain Stewart's brow knitted in puzzlement. 'To what are you referring?' he asked. 'Are you saying that what I saw in that room was something more than a mere child ...'

His host nodded. 'Some beings come from a world beyond our understanding ...' he said quietly.

'You're not talking about a ... a ghost?' Captain Stewart could hardly bring himself to say the word. He was a military man and had never had any time for the supernatural.

His host shook his head slowly. 'Not exactly a ghost,' he said. 'More of a vision. There is a very old tradition in my family that the boy — we call him the Radiant Boy — chooses to appear only to those who will achieve great power.'

Captain Stewart gazed at him with skepticism written all over his face. 'However,' the other man continued almost apologetically, 'It is also part of the tradition that the chosen person ... er ... dies a violent death.'

Stewart threw back his head and laughed. 'I never heard so much rubbish in my life,' he declared.

His host looked at him mournfully. 'The records that have been kept of the Radiant Boy's appearances do seem to confirm this notion ...' he said quietly, as if to himself. But Stewart had already moved away and was helping himself to bacon and eggs.

Captain Stewart spent a pleasant enough morning with his host and hostess. Immediately after lunch, he made his farewells, saddled his horse and galloped fast back to Belfast. He never saw the ancient mansion again.

Several years passed. Captain Stewart did indeed reach dizzying heights of power in the country. Through family influence he succeeded to the House of Lords, becoming Viscount Castlereagh. He became a member of the British Government during the administration of William Pitt, first as Minister for War and then Foreign Secretary during the Napoleonic Wars.

Unfortunately, despite his power, Stewart's insensitive handling of home affairs, his part in bringing in the 1801 Act of Union, and his opposition to the radicalism of the time made him deeply unpopular with the Irish people. He became ill. Just one year after he became Marquis of Londonderry, his mind collapsed. At the age of fifty-three, he committed suicide by slashing his own throat with a razor.

During his funeral procession through the streets of London, the mob cheered loudly as the cortège passed, adding to the ignominy surrounding his name. The strange prophesy of the Radiant Boy, all those years before, had come true after all. Stewart had certainly achieved the heights of influence – yet died violently and in despair.

But it was not only to unpopular members of the British government that the Radiant Child appeared. An old story concerning the famous Robert Emmet, leader of the failed 1803 rebellion, who has given his name to many a landmark in and around Dublin, also features a mention of the same spectre.

By early 1803, Emmet was a prominent figure in the United Irishmen. He had been lying low in France for some time and had recently returned home to Ireland to see if he could invigorate the remnants of the movement, which had lain dormant since the rebellion of 1798. Emmet spent his time moving secretly about the Irish countryside, gathering intelligence and garnering support. During this time, he met with some former United Irishmen leaders who were in hiding.

One evening at a gathering in County Wexford, Emmet met with a group of volunteers in a large house in a remote area of the county. He was sitting beside a window that looked out over the rolling countryside towards a nearby dark stand of trees. As the discussions were going apace, Emmet chanced to glance out. In the centre of the trees was a pale glimmer of light.

'What's that?' he asked one of the others.

'What? Where?' replied the man. When Emmet looked back, the light amongst the trees had gone. No-one else had seen it. Nor did any of the men who were posted about the house on the lookout for British agents report that they'd see anything.

Later that evening, he decided to walk to the ancient grove and investigate what he thought he'd seen. Just as he drew near the spot where the glow had come from, he spotted a faint whitish-blue light, illuminating the surrounding tree trunks and branches. Yes, there it was, coming from right in the centre of the grove. And there was something there too — a child, crouched down amongst the bushes, curled in on itself as though in pain, or weeping with grief.

'Hello?' Emmet paused, then he called again. 'Hello?'

The figure didn't look up. As if from a long way away, Robert Emmet heard faint gasps and sighs as though the child were weeping uncontrollably.

'What is it, child? Can't I help you?' asked the revolutionary.

There was no answer, just the dismal sound of unutterable grief. Somewhere, a nightbird called. Fearing an ambush from his enemies, Emmet instinctively crouched. Immediately, the light winked out, plunging the grove into blackness. The figure and the sound of crying were gone.

Emmet stood and scoured the area but there was nothing to be found — no trace of the mysterious child. Wonderingly, he made his way back to the house and related what he'd seen and heard to his comrades.

The story of Emmet's rebellion in 1803 is now a matter of history. Although Emmet was a passionate patriot and a brilliant strategist, he was no leader; the rising was a haphazard and ill-managed affair that was doomed from the outset. A few former brigades of the United Irishmen regrouped and took a full part, while other brigades went missing. Emmet himself quickly lost control of the Dublin faction, many of whom were either ill-prepared or intent on making mischief. The murder by the mob of Lord Kilwarden, a well-thought-of and humane judge, was the turning point. Emmet tried to call off the rising but, by then, things had gone too far.

When it was quashed, Emmet was branded a rebel and a traitor. He was hunted down, arrested, and taken back to Dublin to stand trial. He made a brilliant and eloquent speech from the dock, which moved many of those who heard it, and which inspired future republicans, including those who took part in the Easter Rising of 1916. He was then found guilty and was sentenced to a violent traitor's death. On a September morning in 1803, Robert Emmet was hanged, drawn and quartered. He had fulfilled the curse of the Radiant Boy.

Several other great families of Ireland were troubled by the sporadic appearances of the mysterious weeping child. Such an appearance is sometimes connected with other ghosts that haunt the houses where it has manifested itself. One of these sites is Wilton Castle, in County Wexford. Once more there is a connection to the rebellion of the United Irishmen in 1798.

The story concerns the Jacobs family who resided in nearby Ballinapierce. Captain Archibald Jacob was supposed to have encountered the Radiant Boy whilst riding through a thicket close to the castle around 1795. A proud and cruel man, Jacob was supposed to have ordered the naked, weeping child off his lands, supposing that he was one of the local children. It was only when a bird called from a bush close by and Jacob turned to look, that the spectre vanished and Captain Jacob knew that he'd faced something supernatural. Though alarmed, he dismissed the incident from his mind.

Captain Jacob rose to great local prominence as a captain of the Vinegar Hill Rangers and, during the time of the 1798 Rebellion, he was a magistrate in Enniscorthy. He lived the good life, attending balls and parties all over the county, but he was renowned as a great bully and tyrant, who beat his servants unmercifully and treated his tenants shabbily.

On his way back from a party at Wilton Castle on 29 December 1836, Captain Jacob was crossing a place known as the Black Stream, halfway between the castle and Clough Mills, when his horse stumbled. The Captain was thrown and fell awkwardly. Later, he was found by servants and brought back to the castle, but his neck had been broken by the fall and he was already dead. Now, Archibald Jacob's ghost is also said to haunt the roads around Wilton Castle.

Whether or not the Radiant Boy actually did appear to all these people is a matter for historical and folkloric conjecture, but the story is certainly a persistent one. There is, however, no suggestion of an origin for the phantom and nobody really knows if he is a ghost in the truest sense of the word — that is, the shade of somebody who has departed this life. It might be that he is more akin to a banshee — a warning emissary from the spirit world to those living, who are touched by the far-reaching hand of Fate ...

Corney

Among Irish ghosts, there are 'characters' – just as there are among the living. Sometimes, certain Irish spectres acquire an almost celebrity status. We have already seen one example of this in the ghost of Frank McKenna, who became a focus of local gatherings in the mountains of Tyrone. Another example might be the ghost of the seamstress Grace Connor from Cork, who became something of a wonder as she conscientiously returned from the grave, to complete work left unfinished. People came from many miles round about to see the spectre of Grace appear at midnight to recommence her sewing. This continued until the orders were complete, whereupon she simply vanished.

Dublin too has had its fair share of celebrity ghosts. In Henrietta Street, for instance, the one-time townhouse of Sir Nicholas Loftus, the first Earl of Ely, acquired a widespread reputation for being haunted by a number of eighteenth-century ghosts. Indeed, the building is still a 'stop' on ghost-walking tours of the city. The theatre in Fishamble Street, too, has attracted attention with spectral appearances along its passageways and galleries, and with strange knockings on the walls of its Green Room. Even Hendrick Street, a Georgian thoroughfare until extensive demolition in the 1960s, was reputedly the home of several well-known spectres. Long-dead residents were seen coming and going from houses, and noises were heard coming from the empty flats at Number 7. Another area of Georgian Dublin, St. Stephen's Green, is said to be teeming with ghosts, from the spectres of serving maids and phantom children haunting the Shelbourne Hotel, to the apparition of Buck Whaley striding down towards Cuffe Street as he might have done when alive.

But perhaps one of the best-known Dublin phantoms is that of an old servant, simply known as 'Corney', who refused to leave the site of his former employment, even in death. Indeed, so famous did Corney become that he excited the attentions of several churches in Dublin and became the subject of letters to the city's newspapers as late as the 1920s. Although his real name has never been revealed, Corney can truly be said to be one of the city's celebrity ghosts. He is, to the best of my knowledge, the only ghost ever to have haunted a coalhole.

What sort of a ghost was Corney? For a start, he is one of the few Irish ghosts who could talk animatedly and reply to questions that were put to him. He also seems to have been extremely intelligent and had a quick sense of humour. Like Frank McKenna, he specialised in prophecy, but Corney also had the ability to make his prognostications entertaining. He was no respecter of rank and showed scant courtesy to 'the great and the good' of Dublin who came to visit him.

Corney also had his darker side and could, if pushed, be violent. Corney was not a 'dangerous ghost' in the correct sense, although the spirit did portray some dangerous elements. There have been some attempts to classify him as a poltergeist – a spirit that throws or breaks household items, or that bites or scratches the living – but this is not wholly accurate. Rather, the spirit combined personality with supernatural manifestations, making him one of Dublin's finest phantoms.

Although widely known and written about in volumes of ghost stories, the address of the house that Corney's ghost inhabited is uncertain. The identity of the family he haunted is also something of a mystery since, in all the accounts, they are simply referred to as the genteel 'A— family', living in a house near St. Stephen's Green.

The A— family was not the first family to live in this house. Some time before, another family had lived there, together with a faithful retainer – an elderly man – who'd died there. The old servant's real name was thought to be Cornelius, but he had been known to one and all as Corney. Corney was said to have been 'a rare oul' character' and was popular both with his employers and with the community in general. A year after his death, the family moved away and the house fell vacant. The A— family took up residence shortly afterwards, in the mid-nineteenth century, and in was then that the disturbances were said to have begun.

Shortly after moving in, Mr. A— sprained his ankle and had to get around by means of a heavy crutch, which he kept at the head of his bed. Late one night, his wife was awakened from a sound sleep, by the sound of something big and awkward moving across the lobby. The sound was a heavy 'thump-thump' and for a moment, she thought that it might be her husband walking with his crutch. However, his crutch was still propped in its spot at the head of the bed. As she looked, the odd sounds in the lobby died away and silence returned.

From then onwards, strange noises were often heard — usually bangings and thumpings around the house. The family simply put this down to 'the old house settling' but Mr A— suspected something very different. He was of the opinion that the place might be haunted. And so it was proved for, after a time, a presence began to make itself known by speaking.

The voice sounded like a man speaking from an empty barrel. It was sepulchral and hollow, but the words could be heard quite distinctly. It seemed to be located mainly in the coal-hole in the kitchen, although from time to time it wandered all over the house, sometimes issuing from cupboards, sometimes from under the beds — and sometimes even from the bread tins!

The ghost that came to be known as Corney was certainly troublesome. He seemed to delight in playing pranks on the household or in embarrassing them in some way. Most of his more malicious jokes were directed towards the servants, whom he tormented regularly. Cups and crockery frequently disappeared, only to turn up again in places where he had hidden them. He relocated food so that no-one could find it. Doors and locks throughout the house were tampered with, so that when keys were turned, they strained and eventually snapped.

In order to get away from the mischievous spirit, some of the servants who slept downstairs in the kitchen asked if they could be relocated at night. Corney, they claimed, was nipping them or reaching under the bedclothes to pull at their toes. He was also extremely noisy and rowdy, preventing them from getting any sleep with his laughter and singing at odd hours of the night. A 'press-up bed' was therefore set up in a room at the top of the house to accommodate a couple of maids who'd been especially terrified. As the girls were about to retire for the night, the doors of the press-up bed were suddenly flung open and Corney's voice exclaimed, 'Ah ha, you devils! I am here before you! Believe me, I'm not confined to any one part of this house!' The two maids were apparently so horror-struck that they fainted clean away, and afterwards sought alternative employment.

For the most part, Corney remained no more than a disembodied voice, invisibly lifting crockery, shaking furniture and generally making his presence felt about the place. Only twice did he take on a recognizable physical shape. Once he appeared to a seven-year-old boy who was related to the A— family. The child described Corney as a naked man, very old, with a curl in the middle of his forehead. The other person who saw him is reported to have died from fright. Other than that, Corney never revealed himself.

On a gloomy afternoon towards the end of the year, one of the servants was preparing a fish for dinner. Leaving it on the table in the kitchen, she went to fetch something else that she needed and when she returned, it had disappeared. Fearing that her master would blame her, she began to cry, whereupon a voice piped up from the coalhole. 'There, you blubbering fool. There is your fish for you!' and almost at once, the fish was flung from the coal-cellar and onto the kitchen floor whilst the place rang with Corney's laughter.

Visitors to the A— family from the country sometimes brought presents of homegrown vegetables, or home-cured bacon. Corney would steal these and hang them out on pieces of string like Christmas decorations. Occasionally, items of fruit and vegetables would disappear, only to re-emerge as ammunition. The visitors would be pelted by rotting foodstuffs by an unseen source. Once he placed a fish from the pantry into a beef-pickling crock, thus spoiling the beef. There was also a certain downstairs press that he wouldn't allow anything to be placed in — if anything was put into it, it would be immediately thrown out onto the floor.

Nor were Corney's activities confined to foodstuffs. He even implicated the servants in theft. On two occasions, a set of silver spoons disappeared from the dining room and couldn't be found. 'The spoons are under the ticking of the servant's bed upstairs!' proclaimed a voice from the coalhole and then proceeded to name the people involved in the alleged removal of the spoons, both of whom were extremely

trustworthy servants of long standing. The spoons were subsequently found where Corney had said they'd be, but it was
decided that it was Corney trying to cause trouble in the
household.

From time to time, the lively spirit's activities would cease
and no voice issued from the coalhole. The entire household
would dare to hope that Corney was gone, but invariably he
would return a few days later, louder and more mischievous
than ever.

After one of these disappearances, one of the family dared
to ask Corney why he had been so quiet — had he gone from
the house?

'When I was alive,' replied the hollow voice, 'I had a daughter and she is still amongst the living. She is married and lives
not far from here.' The spirit named a certain street, close
by. 'I've been to see her for a day or two.'

Based on this information, Mr. A— and a couple of the
servants made investigations in several of the neighbouring
streets. They found no trace of the woman to whom Corney
referred, though they did find people who claimed to have
seen a very old man walking the street, though no-one knew
him or where he went.

'You've been checking up on me,' the voice suddenly
announced after this expedition, 'And your delving has come
to naught! I shall see my daughter when it pleases me.' From
then on, the spirit would often announce that he was 'off to
see the daughter' and would fall silent for several days —

sometimes for as long as a week. In every case, however, Corney came back livelier than ever and the pranks that he played around the house seemed to increase.

By now the ghost was widely known all over Dublin and was the talk of society around St. Stephen's Green. Many people were anxious to visit and talk to Corney for themselves. Consequently, the house thronged with those who wanted to call into the coalhole and hear what they might hear. Corney entertained them all, answering questions that they put to him and displaying knowledge and culture far and above that of an ordinary serving man. He would not, however, answer any questions about either himself or his past life. Only on rare occasions did he make reference to his earthly existence. 'I've been an evil man!' wailed the hollow voice. 'I've lived a cruel life – and I've died the death for it. Take heed from my example!'

The A— family was now at their wits' end as to how to get rid of the troublesome phantom. In desperation, they appealed to a clergyman to come to the house and exorcise Corney. The old gentleman said that he'd visit and assess the situation. He'd come in disguise so that Corney wouldn't know he was a priest and so might answer him more freely.

The priest duly arrived in ordinary clothes and took a seat in the kitchen, beside the coalhole. Conversation drifted back and forth with everyone waiting for Corney to speak or make his presence known, but no sound came from the cellar. In the end, the priest left.

'Corney, why didn't you speak to our guest?' asked an exasperated Mr A—. There was silence for a moment.

'I couldn't speak while that good man was in the house,' answered Corney. 'But listen to me — I will not obey any priest or clergyman, nor will I answer when they are present. Their power is of this world and I am beyond that.'

Mr A— persisted and asked Corney where he might be — was he in Purgatory or on some other plane of existence? This time the voice was slow in answering and when it did, it was low and sad. 'The Great God does not permit me to tell you where I presently am. But rest assured, I was a bad, bad man and I now suffer because of it. Take heed of my plight!'

Within minutes, however, Corney was back to his old self, and proceeded to announce that he, too, was expecting company in the coalhole. 'I'll away to prepare for them,' he declared. 'If you want water out of the soft-water tank you should take it now as my friends and I will be using it.' With that, the voice fell silent.

Later that night, five or six different and distinctive voices were heard to issue from the coalhole, laughing and calling to each other. In the morning, the water in the tank was black and unfit for human consumption. The bread and butter in the pantry had turned mouldy and rancid and were marked and streaked with sooty fingers. This was the only 'party' that Corney had in his coal-cellar but it terrified both the servants and the A— family.

Sometimes, visitors were brought in to question Corney about his previous life. It was hoped that in this way, some means might be found to get rid of him. Corney generally answered evasively and volunteered little information. When he did speak about his past life, it was usually to bemoan the fact that he'd been a bad man and that he was being punished. Usually some sort of pious moralizing about the wickedness of the human condition and a warning to everyone present to follow and uphold 'the Christian life' accompanied this disclosure.

Despite this contrition for past wrongs and his reticence about his own life, Corney was not averse to embarrassing guests by revealing instances from their own past lives of which he appeared to have an intimate knowledge. On one occasion, a medium came to the house to talk to him. Sitting in the kitchen, she concentrated on the coalhole, gently calling out to the recalcitrant spirit. Suddenly the voice burst forth. 'Ha, you old crow! What gives you the right to come to talk to one such as I? You have a daughter living in the town, whom you never acknowledge! Even I, for all my wickedness, acknowledge my own children!' At that the medium, red with embarrassment, fled the house, while Corney roared with laughter from the coal-hole.

On one occasion, Corney was slightly more forthcoming about his past. He claimed he had died in an upstairs room in the house and that this event had 'bound him to the building'. Such a room certainly existed — but it was not the one in which the old servant Cornelius was said to have died. So who was this Corney? Was he the spirit of the old servant, or not? He would not reveal any more details, and the mystery deepened.

Corney continued to make his presence felt. He joined in when people gathered in the kitchen to talk. He would offer opinions on past events or current issues. He made known his particular preferences concerning clothes, food and even people. There wasn't a topic on which he didn't have an opinion and he gave the impression of having been well educated and well read.

Corney was also very forthright. He spoke sneeringly about people he disliked and revelled in embarrassing the proud and the haughty. Once, a rather grand lady visitor was barking instructions at one of the maids when Carney's voice issued from the coal-hole. 'What are you giving yourself airs for, you old baggage? You tell everybody that your father was a peer of the realm, but you and I both know that he was a stable-hand!' Corney went on to name the groom he claimed was the lady's real father. 'Don't go pretending to be a grand lady in front of me, for I know your history full well – and I'll tell more if I have to.' This threat broke off in a great peal of laughter, while the lady hurriedly made her excuses and left.

On another occasion, a venerable clergyman called in to see Mr A—. While he was in the hallway, removing his coat, Corney's voice boomed from inside a grandfather clock, telling ribald jokes and singing vulgar songs, the tone of which brought a blush to the elderly gentleman's cheek. The clergy-man instructed the spirit to be quiet 'in the Name of God' but Corney sang all the louder and became even more bawdy. 'I'll not be commanded by the likes of you, you sanctimonious old clown!' he retorted. 'I'm a person who enjoyed life, not trapped behind a graveyard face like you! Get out of my sight, you old hypocrite, in case I tell everybody what I know about you!' Knowing of Corney's previous disclosures, the clergy-man beat a hasty retreat. 'Run, you pious old fool!' called Corney after him from the clock.

Corney had his favourite targets amongst visitors to the house — usually those whom he could frighten the most. He seemed to dislike those who had no fear of him and wouldn't talk to them. Any questions that they asked or comments they made were usually greeted with a stony silence from the coal-hole.

One uncle, who called at the house regularly, often tried to get him to speak. Exasperated at getting no response, he finally took the kitchen poker and hammered at the door of the coal-cellar, shouting, 'I'll make you speak!' There was no reply and at last he gave up. The next morning, the poker was found in the grate, broken cleanly in two.

'How dare you allow that utter buffoon to disturb my rest?' thundered an angry voice. 'He's an arrogant ape and not worthy of my attention!' Throughout the day, cups were broken, coals fell out of the fire and onto the hearth, and cut-lery went missing as Corney showed his displeasure.

Another rather frequent visitor to the A— household was Uncle Richard, who had absolutely no fear of the spectre. Corney hated Uncle Richard with a passion, disparagingly referring to him as 'Old Four Eyes' because he wore a large set of spectacles. Although he would not speak to Uncle Richard directly, he would call the nickname from the coal-hole whenever the old man passed by and would blow raspberries at him behind his back. One night when Uncle Richard came to stay, he awoke to find that all his bedclothes had been pulled down around his legs and knotted about his feet. 'I slept on good Master Richard's feet all night!' Corney boasted the following day, 'And he didn't even know it!'

Corney's rudeness continued. He greeted the arrival of a minister with the remark, 'Who let that sanctimonious black crow into the house?' He referred to another minister's 'tombstone face', and told a lady visitor that she had 'a countenance like a spoiled spaniel'. Each comment was accompanied by gusts of devilish laughter, which those present didn't share.

Not surprisingly, perhaps, given his air of self-importance, Corney was extremely susceptible to flattery, and Mrs A— often used to get the better of him by coaxing him. 'You've a very fine voice, Corney,' she'd say cajolingly when guests were due to visit. 'Very rich and vigorous. I love to listen to it — but wouldn't it be even finer if you'd rest it for a time? Would you not do that for my sake?' The pompous ghost would invariably agree and, for a time, conversations could carry on in peace and without interruption.

As time passed Corney became more boisterous and uncontrollable. Late in the night or early in the morning, his voice would keep everyone awake, as he sang bawdy songs or recited dubious rhymes. He was just as troublesome during the day. Knockings and rattlings filled the place, burning coals were tossed out of the fire, and crockery was thrown from the cupboards. He was creating mayhem and uproar in an already tired and weary household and the situation was rapidly becoming intolerable. Finally, Mr A— decided to sell the house.

There was a problem, however. Corney's reputation now extended all across Dublin and, consequently, few buyers were interested in the property. Those hardy souls who decided to come and view the dwelling were treated to such barrages of abuse and insult from the coal-hole, that most fled in terror. Those who persisted were humiliated further, as Corney revealed intimate (and usually accurate) details about their private lives.

'You old miser, with your face like a midden,' he screamed at one viewer. 'What brings you creeping around here when you know you can't afford the asking price? You and I know that you're in debt to the bank, so get out of my sight with your hideous face!' Gradually possible purchasers faded away all together.

One day, Mr A— had a frightening thought. With trepidation, he asked Corney if he were planning to follow them to another part of the city if they did somehow manage to sell the house. To Mr A—'s relief, Corney admitted that he couldn't leave the site: 'I am tied to this building where I died.' But, he assured them, 'Even if they throw down this house, I will remain and trouble the very stones!'

Although this declaration gave the A— family some reassurance, it didn't help them in selling the place. In desperation, Mrs A— appealed to the spirit to keep quiet and not to injure or insult those who came to view. Corney eventually promised that he would behave. In the meantime, however, he became increasingly demanding towards the family as they made plans to leave him. He whistled and sang from his coalhole as soon as they were asleep. He would call 'Wake up! Wake up! I'm desirous of some company and conversation. Wake up!' He would make rattling noises everywhere in the house until the family was at its wits' end. The whole thing was intolerable.

The end of their torment, however, was in sight. Late one evening, Corney announced in his customary forthright manner: 'Mrs A—, you'll be alright now. All your troubles will soon be over for I see a lady in black coming up the street to this house and she'll buy it. I'll not stand in her way.' Within half an hour, a widow called and, after discussing terms, agreed to purchase the house. The A— family moved out with all haste to another part of Dublin.

In the days leading to their departure, Corney was remarkably quiet both at night and during the day. The family even joked about it.

'Perhaps he's fretting about us leaving,' said Mr A— with a nervous laugh. He even called into the coal-hole, 'Will you miss us, Corney?' — but there was no answer from him, nor ever any more noise from him again. As the family closed the front door of the tormented house behind them, it felt as though Corney had also left the building.

And there the story of the famous Corney comes to an end. If the widow was troubled by a strange voice in her coal-hole, she never spoke about it. Casual callers were not allowed in and nobody could ascertain whether the spirit was still there. Nothing more was heard about him.

Several years later, the widow herself sold up and moved away and the rundown old house passed through various hands. It was still standing in the 1920s, but has long since gone, demolished amid the rampant development of central Dublin. And what happened to Corney? Could it be that he still causes havoc in one of the modern office blocks around St. Stephen's Green?

Haunted Places

A Night at the 'Ram's Horn'

On a cold afternoon in 2002, high in the mountains of County Derry, a group of men finally demolished the remnants of an old stone wall – all that remained of an ancient house known locally as 'Ram's Horn'. Although it was a private property, some of the original stonework was said to have been part of an ancient coaching inn, giving the place a strong link with former times. It had stood on the site for about 200 years and, in its heyday, had been a stop for travellers on the Belfast–Derry route. Yet in its latter days as a hostelry, there was nothing restful or welcoming about the Ram's Horn. Around the beginning of the nineteenth century, it became a spot where highwaymen and cutthroats gathered, and its name had become a local byword for murder and robbery.

There were also whispers about an even older, darker past. Some claimed that the Ram's Horn had been built on one of the pagan forts that dominated the region – and that some of that antique evil had seeped into its very stones. At some point, someone had incised a rough crucifix into the lintel above the door – perhaps to contain spirits within the place, thus protecting the countryside round about. In any case, despite its being the only hostelry for miles around on a bleak and arduous route, the inn was widely avoided and considered to be a site of both actual and supernatural dread.

Until the mid-1800s, the only ways to travel any distance across Ireland were on foot, on horseback or by coach. Roads were extremely poor and were badly maintained and journeys tended to be long, arduous and uncomfortable. Facilities along the road varied widely, from well-appointed inns to low taverns and squalid 'shebeens' (or illegal drinking houses that sometimes provided lodgings). Passengers crammed into a stuffy, smelly vehicle, however, were usually glad of a break from their travels, no matter how unprepossessing their stop might be.

The proprietors of such taverns were sometimes just as unsavoury as the establishments they ran. Many were in league with the rogues and robbers along the road, and it was not unknown for a passenger to be robbed and murdered somewhere in the wilderness – sometimes with the collusion of the coachman himself. In remote areas, there was little law enforcement, and a great number of crimes went unsolved. Small wonder then that most people didn't venture too far from home unless they really had to.

The main coaching road between Coleraine and Derry – which, today, still bears the sinister name of the 'Murderhole Road' – led across the remote and dangerous Limavady Mountain. Once a coach pulled away from the busy market town of Coleraine, it faced bleak and mountainous territory, where thick forests impinged upon deep and desolate bogs as the route started to climb up the mountain itself. There were no real towns on the uplands, only a few isolated hamlets and scattered houses where the people were wary of travellers. In the late 1700s and early 1800s, at least six separate highwaymen and two outlaw gangs operated along the Murderhole Road, robbing and killing travellers at will. It was a brave person who would 'chance the mountain', especially in the short days of winter when bad weather made the roads difficult. Nevertheless, there were a number of inns and hostelries along the mountain road. Most of these were little more than thatched hovels but there was the occasionally fairly large two-storey building where coach passengers might stay the night. The Ram's Horn was one such building.

Built out of dark local stone and with a brick chimney, the inn stood on a particularly lonely stretch of road where the bare and boggy slopes met the forest. On the very edge of the road that straggled over the mountain, it provided a grim resting place before the final push to the top. Through the dark and rain of a winter's night, a light would shine in the small window of the Ram's Horn, guiding coaches and their passengers – to what? Robbery? Death? Something worse? Whatever secrets the sinister inn held have been swept away with the last stone that the workmen discarded, yet its reputation lives on in local tradition. Even today with the last of its stones gone, some local people won't go near the site for fear of what still lurks there …

The traveller looked distastefully at the dilapidated building. At the end of a short, rough lane, close to a stand of gloomy trees, it was not quite what he'd expected – in fact, in the evening light, he wasn't even sure if it was an inn. His sway-backed old horse actually seemed to slow as it approached the place and he wondered if he should turn around and continue his journey over the mountain without halting for the night. He decided against it.

It was 1807 and the times were still unsettled. Although the rebellions of the United Irishmen had failed, remnants of old militias and former sympathisers still roamed the roads. Outlawry and violence still prevailed in remote areas, and this northerly section of the Limavady Mountain was said to have more than its share of them. Besides, night was falling across the bleak countryside, the rising wind was hinting at rain and there was no other shelter.

Once there had been many more living along this road, but famine and poverty had driven the people to an early grave or across the sea to another life. Only the ruins of houses with fallen-in roofs marked their passing. Nowadays the nearest inhabited place was the hamlet of Ringsend, a scattering of small houses tucked away across the neighbouring hills. But on this road there was nothing, just forest and mountain — and the Ram's Horn.

A lantern swung over the doorway of the inn. Its feeble light gave the place a jaundiced aspect that was far from inviting. The traveller felt his horse grow skittish and again he toyed with the notion of turning the animal round and heading on up the mountain. The first flecks of rain, however, made up his mind for him. There was a downpour coming, and it wouldn't be wise to be caught in the open. Better to take his chances at the dirty-looking inn ahead.

The traveller had already heard about the Ram's Horn and its poor reputation in Coleraine. He knew it was a former hangout for poteen-makers, thieves, highwaymen — and even murderers. But that had all been a long time ago and those days were surely past. After a vicious footpad, known as Cushy Glen, had been killed along this road some years before, things had gone very quiet. The inn was surely as peaceful as the countryside around it and safe enough to lodge in for the night.

And yet as he approached the place, the mountain night seemed to grow perceptibly colder. It was as if the building itself drew all the heat from the air around it and he found himself shivering slightly. The curious mixture of lights — the fading daylight and the glow from the lantern in the wall bracket — concentrated odd shadows about the place whilst the dark of the trees coupled with the blank greyness of the walls gave it an eerie appearance. Swallowing nervously, the traveller dismounted and made his way over to the drab wooden door set deep into the stonework beneath the hanging lantern. He tried the latch. It lifted but the door remained closed. It was probably held in place by a bar on the other side. Raising his fist, the traveller struck loudly on the weathered wood.

'Hello in there!' he called. 'Will anybody open this door to a poor traveller?'

A faint blur of rain was carried down on the mountain wind, catching the edge of his coat, but from inside the building there was no answer. The traveller banged on the door again.

'Open up! The night and the weather are both closing in and I've a mind to sit in the comfort beside a blazing fire. Open up!'

Still there was no answer except for a crow, which flew from the brick chimney, disturbed by the noise. He looked upward to follow it but saw only the lowering sky overhead and the grim, grey stonework of the building. And crudely incised into the lintel above, he saw a rough cross. The sight of it gave him no comfort. Then, from beyond the door came a sound – like somebody approaching with slow footsteps.

'Hello?' the traveller called. This time there was a reply.

'Wait a moment,' a voice answered. 'The door's bolted!'

It was an old voice, creaky and full of catches – the traveller couldn't even make out whether it belonged to a man or a woman. There was a rattling noise and he thought that he heard chains being unlocked. The door swung inward.

The face that looked out on the evening was that of a very old man. Grey-yellow hair was hung about the lined and weather-beaten face in matted tresses. His nose was hooked like the beak of a predatory bird and the eyes that regarded the stranger in the doorway were dark and suspicious. The rest of the figure in the shadows of the doorpost was small and thin. He wore a heavy, coarse shirt and a pair of formerly white breeches that were now stained and marked with grime and mud and goodness knew what else. A scrawny hand held a small lamp aloft whilst the eyes darted from side to side around the doorway, as if making sure the traveller was alone.

'Who's there?' The question was asked in a sharp, peevish tone as if the enquirer was angry at being disturbed. 'Who is it?'

'A traveller seeking shelter. This is the Ram's Horn, is it not?' The other looked at the traveller long and hard before replying.

'It is. But it's late and there are no rooms ready.' And with that, the old man made as if to close the door in the traveller's face.

The traveller stared in astonishment. He'd been told that mountainy people could appear unfriendly but he'd never expected a welcome like this! He put his foot out to wedge open the door.

'Wait a minute!' he said, 'What do you expect me to do?'

'There's a place further on in the mountain, near Ringsend, where you might get lodgings for the night,' creaked the figure on the other side of the lamp, grudgingly opening the door again. 'You'd be better off going there. There's nothing here!'

'But Ringsend is miles away,' said the traveller looking upwards towards the brooding sky. 'And there's a storm coming. I'll be caught in a downpour before I get there. The Ram's Horn *is* an inn, isn't it — giving shelter for the night?'

The old man's eyes regarded him coldly.

'It *used* to be an inn,' the odd voice replied slowly. 'But the road over the mountain is far less travelled than it was in the old days and few people stop here'.

The traveller sighed, his patience finally exhausted by the other's lack of basic hospitality.

'Look,' he snapped. 'I'll pay you double what you usually charge for a room, and all I ask for is a seat beside the fire.' The other's eyes shone greedily. The traveller's strategy had worked.

'Then you'd better come in, sir. Just remember that it's upon your own head.'

Wondering what on earth the man could mean, the traveller stepped through and into a large stone hallway that took up the entire length of the building. It was dark, gloomy and incredibly cold — as cold as the bare mountain outside — but a fire burned in the stone fireplace set into the wall. Smoke billowed around the lip of the grate, making the air harsh and acrid. Firelight mingled with the wan glow from candles that were set in niches around the bare stone walls.

Set in front of the fire was an old-fashioned, stiff-backed wooden bench with high sides. Beyond that was a plain oak table with an ordinary low chair pushed in against it, and still further back, several wooden kegs and barrels, draped in all manner of rubbish, rose out of the poor light. What lay beyond these the traveller couldn't quite make out, but it looked like old wooden trunks that spilled rags and clothes onto the stone-flagged floor. His host followed him in from the door with a slightly uneven step.

'It's cold in here and the fire's poor,' he acknowledged. 'I'd give you a room but they're worse — nobody's been in them for years and they're full of damp.' The old man bent forward and lowered his voice almost confidentially. 'I'm sure that you've heard – this place has a bad name. There's supposed to be ... things in some of the rooms, and there are those that have stayed in them who have been found wandering across the mountain with their minds gone.' He lowered his voice even further till it was no more than a whisper. 'Sometimes when I'm here at night on my own, I think I hear a child crying or glasses clinking behind the doors. But there's nothing there – or so I tell myself.'

The old man straightened up again and resumed a normal tone. 'It's strange how your mind can play tricks when you're alone and in an old place – isn't that right, sir?'

The traveller swallowed hard. Just for a moment, he felt slightly unsure of himself.

'I–I suppose it is,' he faltered. 'Don't bother about any of the rooms. I can sleep in this chair as well as any bed!' He instinctively stretched out his hands towards the paltry blaze. 'It's better than facing the mountain, I can assure you. Now, if you'll see to my horse, I'll just settle myself here for the night. Can you see to it yourself or is there an ostler?'

The other shuffled off to his left, across the stone floor. 'There's none here but myself, sir,' he answered. 'Jabez Mullan's my name and I'm the master of this place now. It's a hard and lonely life here now – nobody stops here any more, so I've little money to employ staff. What I can do, I do myself. So I'll see to your horse, sir?'

The traveller nodded. Into the dank chill of the old place, the fire threw out a faint warmth. Now that he was settled, he preferred to stay where he was.

'Sit here for a while, then,' said Mullan, 'And when I come back I'll make you something to eat — though there's not great choice in the way of food ...'

'Please don't bother on my account,' the traveller protested. 'I dined well enough before I left Coleraine. A seat in front of your fire for the night'll be enough.'

Taking the hint, his host shambled forward and began to gather up some broken branches near the hearth to toss onto the fire.

The traveller chuckled drowsily. 'You mentioned the Ram's Horn's reputation and atmosphere. Is the place supposed to be ... haunted maybe?' He had chosen his words carefully, but looked up to find Mullan regarding him coldly.

'There's people that'll tell you they've seen ... things,' he said, 'And so they might've. Who knows? It is not for me to judge. All I know is this place is very remote, and enough loneliness can drive you mad.'

Was it the traveller's imagination or did the queer innkeeper cast a furtive glance into the dark shadows of the room beyond the flickering glow of the fire?

'Your name, now,' the traveller began again, trying to change the subject, 'It's a curious one, isn't it?' High up on the bare stone wall above the fireplace, strange shapes seemed to dance, caused no doubt by the burning sticks below. 'Are you a local man?'

'Mullan's a common enough name around Ringsend and Benbradagh, sir, which is where my mother came from. There's scores of Mullans living up there.' The old man licked his thin lips. 'They say that the Mullans were old kings and priests over by Benbradagh Peak.'

'It's your ... Christian name that intrigued me,' the travel-ler went on. 'Jabez must be an English name, and yet I thought that Ringsend was a fearfully Irish place.'

'My "Christian" name?' replied Mullan. 'It was the name my mother gave me, sir. I was born in this very inn.'

The traveller leaned forward, sensing that he was going to hear more.

'My mother came here to work for a man called Luther Todd,' continued the old man. 'He owned the Ram's Horn at that time — and he was an Englishman. They say my father came from Ringsend but I never knew him. The man Todd looked after us both ...'

His listener began to suspect that the years of loneliness in this isolated place were taking their toll and that Jabez Mullan was grateful for someone to talk to.

'And was it an odd place even in those days?' the traveller asked, trying to draw out his host.

Jabez Mullan hesitated. 'The people round here still talk about it. They said things about the man Todd — that he was in with the highwaymen and that they drank here; that he'd secret rooms built in to the mountain where they could hide!' Mullan cackled. 'All nonsense! If he did, sir, I've never found them. It's true he never turned any away as long as their money was good — but he wasn't a criminal himself.'

Mullan stretched his own calloused hands towards the growing blaze.

'He was murdered when I was just a boy,' he said bleakly. 'They said that it was highwaymen from Ringsend that did it — a falling-out or something, the times were very bad then. My mother and I had gone to Coleraine and didn't get back until that evening. The place had been ransacked, sir, and he'd been hanged from one these beams over the fire.'

Mullan pointed upwards. 'Some said that the robbers came in and surprised him. Some said that there'd been a quarrel about loot. That's what the military from Coleraine said anyway. I was just a boy at the time. Some people thought that it was his neigbours that did it, for he wasn't that well liked.'

Mullan looked deep into the flames of the fire. 'Some say that his ghost still haunts the place, but I've never seen it.' He paused. 'I'd better see to your horse, sir.' And, with that, he went hobbling off into the dark.

The traveller waited. Stealthy shadows, distorted by the spluttering light of the candles, began to crowd around him and, as the fire started up in the grate, it seemed to create more. They glided round him to form knots of darkness in the corners close to the chimney breast. He started up. Out of the corner of his eye, he thought that someone — or something — had just run quickly behind the high back of his seat, just out of his line of vision. There was something else, too.

He could swear that he heard a low whispering.

'Hello, Mullan?' called the traveller into the dark, though he knew in his heart that the old man would never have been able to stable his horse so quickly.

The whispering steadily increased — feathery sounds that were gone almost as soon as he was sure he'd heard something. He thought that there were words mingled amongst them but he couldn't really make them out.

'Hello?' he said again. 'Is anybody there?'

The sounds seemed to be coming from the gloom behind him, from the dark corners of the room but, turning round and squinting, he found the shapes too vague to make anything out. The traveller turned back to the fire.

'It's Mullan's queer story,' he murmured to himself. 'And I must be exhausted.'

The strange light in the huge room — a mixture of candlelight and firelight— flickered eerily along the wall, making strange shapes on it. The traveller found his gaze wandering back to the bare patch of wall, high up to the right of the fireplace, where the dancing shadows seemed most distorted. Was it his imagination or was the outline of a dancing figure again taking shape before his eyes? A figure turning and spinning in the firelight? A figure with a rope around its neck ...

The traveller sat up and shook his head vigorously.

'This is the result of Mullan's silly stories,' he growled. 'I'm letting my imagination run away with me.' Yet he could see the outline, appearing to grow more and more distinct as the seconds passed. 'It's just my own fancy,' he repeated aloud. 'There's nothing there — nothing at all.'

Suddenly the traveller felt a tug at the sleeve of his coat. He turned sharply. There was nothing there. Yet he could have sworn that something had touched him — he had distinctly felt it. The fire crackled and spat but the traveller was now feeling that there was nothing either homely or reassuring about the sound. He rubbed his eyes. All he needed was a good sleep. But even as he formed the thought, there was another definite movement in the gloom behind him. He span round. Jabez Mullan stood in the doorway.

'Your horse is fed and stabled, sir,' he said. 'Maybe it's as well that you didn't chance the mountain tonight for there's a deal of rain and I see a fog of some sort starting to come together a little ways further up.'

The old man spoke with a repressed excitement, which the traveller thought a strange reaction to the fog's approach. Perhaps the strange old man liked the inn to be completely cut off.

Suddenly, the traveller jumped, as if startled. 'Did you hear that?' he said.

'Hear what?' replied the other.

'That whispering sound …?'

'No, sir,' said Mullan smoothly. 'Now, are you sure that I can't get you something to eat? You're welcome to share what I have.'

The traveller waved the offer away and the landlord stooped to tend to the fire once more. Behind them in the dark, it seemed that the whispering was growing in intensity, but Jabez Mullan remained untroubled by it.

The traveller tried to take his mind off the insidious sound. 'You were telling me about the previous owners of this place?'

Mullan looked up from the fire. 'Ah yes. Well, long before Todd's time there was a woman here, sir. And a wicked woman she was, by all accounts. Scotch. Name of Tibby Fawe. People said that she was a witch with the power t'raise old spirits. She may have even built the Ram's Horn herself on this spot for that reason — it is the site of an old pagan place of worship, y'see.'

The traveller nodded.

'Oh, yes, a wicked woman,' Mullan continued dreamily. 'Her and her son lived here — muddled in his mind, he was, but very, very strong. They say that the two of them murdered folk who came to stay here and buried their bodies up in the mountain.'

The traveller heard the whispering behind them growing very insistent — and there were new sounds too, like the scurrying of rats or mice. Despite the crackling fire, he felt cold.

'But there's worse, sir! They say that Tibby Fawe practised witchcraft and that she used some of the bodies in … horrible practices.'

The traveller swallowed audibly. Part of him did not want to hear any more, but part of him was fascinated. 'And what became of this ... witch-woman?' he wavered. Again he thought he felt something reach round his chair and tug at his sleeve. And then it was gone.

Mullan shook his head. 'Nobody can rightly say, sir,' he replied. 'She and her son just disappeared one night. Some say that they got lost on the mountain and died, some say that they fled to avoid the law, and some that the son killed the mother and then fled. Others'll tell you that the Devil came for them both.' Mullan cast a furtive glance into the shadows. 'They'll tell you too that their ghosts still haunt this place — strangling people, like they did in times gone by.'

Raising his eyes, the traveller looked towards the blank space above the fire — it was empty. No shadow dangled there. The whole thing, he imagined, had been nothing more than a fancy.

Suddenly, Mullan cocked his head. 'Did you hear that, sir?'

The traveller listened but could hear nothing over the scuffling and whispering in the background gloom.

'Is it, perhaps, the wind in all the trees around the property?' he asked hopefully.

His host straightened himself and peered uncertainly into the gloom. 'I thought it was a voice,' he mumbled. 'Somebody calling. Maybe another traveller out on the mountain, round the back of the inn. I'll go and see — settle my mind.' And with his awkward step, he disappeared into the murk.

'I'll be only a moment!' he called back. 'There it is again — I'm sure it was a voice. Somebody lost in the storm ...' The last words trailed away, and then he was gone — swallowed up by the darkness that seemed to creep across the stone-flagged floor.

The traveller waited to hear the sound of a door closing but none came. Only the snap and crack of the fire in the grate. His eyes wandered back to the patch of bare stonework above the fire. The odd light had once again played its trick, and the shadows were again dancing, forming into the shape of a man with a noose around his neck, spinning in the wind ...

From behind the chair, something tugged sharply at his sleeve and then darted back into the blackness. As the traveller stared around him, the fire suddenly flared wildly and fell away. The traveller squashed his rising fears, sat back and closed his tired eyes for a second.

When he opened them again, it seemed to be some time later, for the light had changed. There were more lanterns and candles, a low table had been placed between him and the blaze, and several chairs were drawn up on the other side.

On the chairs, sat three evil-looking men. Two of them had narrow, feral faces that squinted aggressively towards him across the firelight. The third, also looking in his direction, was very badly scarred. On a low sutty-stool between them all sat an old crone with a bit of coarse cloth tied about her head like a scarf, and a crude pipe wedged firmly between her toothless gums. Greasy, black hair escaped from under the head covering, falling down to her thin shoulders. Her hollow eyes were deepest black and she, too, stared at the traveller with almost palpable hostility. In the shadows, seated near the chimney breast, loomed the monstrous outline of a huge, overgrown boy. He was picking scraps of bloody meat from a tin plate on his lap with a slow, awkward motion.

Even though he knew it to be impossible, the traveller had no doubt that he was looking at Tibby Fawe and her weak-minded son, together with some of their evil guests. He opened his mouth to call out, but no sound would come. To his horror, he found he was paralysed and unable to move from his seat.

One of the narrow-faced men lifted a creaky fiddle and began to play tunelessly — the traveller heard the distorted sound as if it were echoing from far away. He could also hear the whisperings of the hag on the other side of the hearth. She seemed to be muttering urgently to the others, the pipe moving up and down in the corner of her mouth. Although he could not hear what she said, he knew she was talking about him, for the men kept glancing at him and at each other. A feeling of panic swamped him as he struggled pointlessly in his seat.

Leaning forward, the scarred man reached down into his boot and produced a long-bladed knife, grinning at the hor-rified traveller opposite. Meditatively, he tested its sharpness between his thumb and forefinger. A drop of blood glistened in the firelight. Tibby Fawe quickly leaned over, snatched the man's hand and licked the blood off. Then she whispered something to him, making descriptive gestures in the traveller's direction that she did not trouble to conceal.

Summoning all his strength, the traveller again tried to shout. 'Mullan! Jabez Mullan!' But his efforts only produced a harsh croak as the name died in his throat. The horrid gathering on the other side of the table threw back their heads in distant laughter.

On the flagstones by the fire, the traveller noticed the blood-streaked tin plate lying discarded, and he realised that Tibby's weak-minded son was right behind him. At that moment, an enormous pair of hands reached round and grabbed him about the throat.

As the traveller gagged and choked and shuddered, trying to shake off the grip of the monster, the ghostly gathering leapt to their feet and again howled with laughter. The pressure on his neck increased. As the traveller twisted and turned his head, his frantic gaze settled on the stretch of stonework above the fire. This time there was no mistake. The shadow was back, so clear that the traveller could see the whites of Luther Todd's eyes rolling back as he danced toward his death on the end of the rope.

'Look!' The word was felt rather than heard. 'Look up there!' Tibby Fawe was pointing towards the shadow. ' That's your fate, too! What befell Luther Todd will befall you this night!' With that, the company roared and danced with a fiendish glee.

The traveller felt the pressure on his neck slacken for an instant. Desperate, and realising he was looking into the face of death, he called on his last reserves of strength. Suddenly finding his voice, he screamed, 'In the Name of God!'

The effect on the company was dramatic. At the mention of the Holy Name, Tibby Fawe, her son and the three vile men all fell to their knees wringing their hand and howling. 'In the Name of God!' shouted the traveller again. In front of his very eyes the awful vision in front of him rippled — and then vanished, leaving darkness and firelight in its wake.

With another cry, he sprang from his chair and ran gibbering over the stone-flagged floor towards the inn door, as if pursued by demons. As he ran, his ears were filled with whispering, and he fought off something invisible that dragged relentlessly at his arms.

'Mullan!' he sobbed, 'Where are you?'

There was no answer. In front of him, the inn door hung from its hinges, bordered by weeds and nettles. Dashing through, he found his horse grazing under a tree nearby and, without thinking, he threw himself awkwardly into the saddle. Around him, the wind shrieked like the howling of Tibby Fawe and her horrid friends. Rain slapped his face like a wet fist but he didn't care. He didn't care about anything but to be away from that hellish place. He urged his horse on into the dark and storm as fast as it would go.

* * *

The hamlet of Ringsend was no more than a huddle of several low, mean thatched houses, clustered in the shelter of the mountain's upper slopes. Most of the dwellings were in darkness, their owners long in bed. Even so, a black iron lantern still glimmered in the window of a small shebeen halfway along the track that served as a village street. Leaping from his mount, the traveller hammered on the barred door of the place.

'Hello! Hello! Open up! Please open up!' His voice carried an edge of hysteria. Bolts were drawn back and a sleepy landlady looked out, roused by his frantic knocking. 'Let me in! For God's sake, let me in!' He stumbled past her into the small house whist the woman stood gape-mouthed.

'What is it that ails ye?' she at last found her voice. 'Is it something out on the mountain road?' Finding a rough seat, he spilled out his story — the strange innkeeper, the terrible vision of a man hanging from the rafters, his ghastly encounter with Tibby Fawe and her evil guests, the ghostly and menacing atmosphere of the Ram's Horn. She stared at him in disbelief.

'But sir,' she eventually said, 'The Ram's Horn's a near ruin — abandoned. The land round about's been bought over by a man from Derry City but he's done nothing with the old inn, just left it to rot. It's falling down. There's no shelter to be had there. You must have stayed somewhere else and had a bad dream. Were you over in Shanlongford perhaps?'

The traveller shook his head vehemently. 'No! it was the Ram's Horn! The landlord was Jabez Mullan ...'

The woman shook her head in her turn. 'That place is but a shell, sir. Boarded up and left to rot. There was a Jabez Mullan there all right, but he's long dead. He lies over in an old churchyard near Articlave. A dark man he was, born of dark blood. I heard my grandfather speak of him many a time. They found him hanging from a rafter in that old place, just as they found the previous landlord, the man that brought him up — Todd his name was. History repeating itself. No-one ever knew why they did it. No, you won't have seen Jabez Mullan, sir, not in this world anyway.'

She paused and looked at him piercingly. 'And Tibby Fawe's been dead even longer, though nobody knows where she's buried. It was all but a bad dream, sir.'

The woman went behind the low counter in the corner of the room. 'Are you all right, sir? Here, you look very frightened and cold, and you've gone very white. I'll get you a drink — put the warmth back in your bones.'

'Mullan's dead for years?' the traveller stammered. 'But I spoke to Mullan this very night and he was sitting there as real as you are. And the Ram's Horn is ruined and boarded up? It's a rough, cold place, to be sure, but it was still habitable. I was there. There was a fire...'

She looked at him queerly.

'No, sir. None lives at the Ram's Horn. It must've been some other place. And you couldn't have spoken with Jabez Mullan — unless you can talk to the dead.'

A chill began to creep up the traveller's back.

'My husband,' the woman continued, 'can take you to where he lies — cold and in the clay.' Her guest looked at her blankly, shivering with more than the chill of the creeping dawn light.

Later that morning, the traveller returned along the road with the innkeeper's husband. To his right was the familiar stand of dark trees, alive with crows that sailed up and down on the breeze. The short laneway was still there, though more overgrown and potholed than he'd remembered from the previous night. His horse still moved uneasily down towards the trees, and the other man kept well behind him. As they drew nearer, the traveller saw the low building of the night before, close to the stand of trees. Beyond it the land stretched away, hard and sour, to the mountain heights.

The traveller dismounted and saw clearly that the dwelling ahead was in ruins, with its upper storey open to the elements. It was obvious that the place had been uninhabited for many long years.

'There y'are, sir,' said the Ringsend man. 'That's all that's left o' the Ram's Horn.'

The traveller looked over the grey stone walls, green with climbing ivy and weeds; the crumbling chimney; the gaping window frames; the empty doorway. He knew that nobody could possibly live there. And yet there was the niche in the stonework where the lantern had hung and there was the incised cross in the lintel above the now-doorless doorway.

'It was a great inn in its time,' the other continued. 'They say that it might open again as an inn or a private house, but that's not the wish of the locals. Better that it's left t'fall down on its own.' And he spat from the saddle of his horse into a clump of bushes. 'Bad cess to it!'

The traveller continued to gaze at the ruin and a crow, perched on the ruined gable returned his gaze with a sharp and beady eye. Were his wits deserting him? Just what had he seen the night before? Some madness brought on by the evil atmosphere of the ruin in front of him?

'Where was I?' he asked wonderingly, fearing for his sanity.

The other shrugged thin shoulders.

'Who can say, sir?' he answered, his tone softening a little. 'Some people imagine things on these uplands. But there's some'll tell ye that old powers and ghosts sometimes manifest themselves t'them that are willin' t'see. Always in places cursed by old wickedness.' He gave a slightly nervous laugh. 'But it was probably all a dream. Stranger things have happened.'

Somewhere across the mountain, a bird called with a cackling laugh — like a lost, mad soul crying out to them. The traveller shuddered again as he relived the horrors of the previous night.

'Yes,' he said softly, 'Stranger things have happened.'

The White Lady of Kilcosgriff

Many of the ancient, aristocratic families of Ireland claim to be followed by warning ghosts, which signal a forthcoming death amongst their relatives. In the Ireland of not so long ago, this was considered to be a mark of status; it indicated a venerable lineage from the Gaelic past. The notion of the banshee – a wailing creature which allegedly follows many families with either 'O' or 'Mac' in their names – is a well-known Irish motif and needs little expansion here.

But the banshee is not the only death-foretelling messenger in Ireland's ghost lore. In times past, many families believed they had their own specific spirit, usually a long-dead ancestor who watched over the clan, and predicted the deaths of family members. This, of course, was a variation of the old Celtic belief that the dead still took an interest in the affairs of the living, and intervened in order to give warnings or advice.

There were many folkloric variants of this central premise, mainly to do with a ghost's motivation for issuing the warning. There are two types of warning ghost: the first warns out of an altruistic impulse, to prepare the family for a tragedy; the second warns as a form of baleful gloating over a traditional enemy. In both cases, the spectre appears to family members immediately prior to a death.

These death-presaging phantoms are often connected with symbols of a vanished grandeur, such as stately homes or castles. One such tale, which conforms to many of the motifs of Celtic ghostlore, comes from Kilcosgriff Castle in County Limerick. The story dates from around the mid-eighteenth century, and the circumstances surrounding the exact origins of the ghosts in question are extremely curious ...

'Upon your own head be it,' said the lame old man from his seat at the corner of the fireplace. 'But I wouldn't take a soldier's pension to set foot in yon Haunted Room, and that's a fact!' The cripple leaned forward heavily on his stick and spat messily into the blaze beside him. 'But, young Master, if you want to take a chance with the ghost there, 'tis up t'yourself!'

With that the old man drew back into the shadows of the large stone mantelpiece. His eerie warning made William Langford feel uneasy and, for the first time since his discharge from the army, the young man experienced the unwelcome creep of fear along his spine.

'What do you know about what supposedly haunts the room, Patrick?' he enquired, trying to maintain an air of nonchalant bravado. The lame man shifted awkwardly on his seat.

'I couldn't rightly say, Master William,' he admitted. 'For there's so many stories about it. But I know that the room's badly haunted all right'.

William continued to look at him as the old man self-consciously cleared his throat and continued. 'Nobody can rightly say the manner of spirit it might be, for nobody's spent overlong in that particular chamber. Some say that it's the ghost of a man — a bad old squire from the Plantation times; others'll tell ye that it's the spirit of a lady, though none can say where she's from. I've heard too that it's a young gallant — not unlike yourself, sir. One of your own ancestors, maybe? But who's to know the real truth — and who would want to find out …?' Old Patrick looked meaningfully at the young man but would say no more.

The two were sitting in the great barn-like kitchen of Kilcosgriff Castle — an old, rambling structure in a poor state of repair, where William's family, the Coplen-Langfords, had lived for centuries. Old Patrick Farrell had been a servant there for a long time — so long that he was almost a member of the family itself — and he was said to know many of the old place's secrets. But, like many of the Irish servants, he refused to talk about them, preferring to keep what knowledge he had about the castle to himself. The stubborn old fellow, William thought crossly, wouldn't even discuss it with a scion of the very family that he served!

As a child, the young man had heard of the Haunted Room, which was located at the end of a long, shadowy, portrait-hung corridor. He also knew that few people would sleep there. Of the few that had, it was said that they had experienced a restlessness and disturbance the whole night through. However, if any of them had actually seen anything — and William doubted that they had — they wouldn't talk about it the following day. Thus the so-called Haunted Room retained its air of mystery and supernatural dread. Not even the maids would light a fire in its grate after dark, or answer the summoning bell that was said to ring down in the servant's quarters from time to time. They believed that a ghostly hand pulled the bell-rope ...

William had heard very vague and garbled accounts of the ghost who stalked in its shadows. Some said that it was a tall, languid, indistinct figure that seemed to be poring over some sort of book or scroll; others swore that it was a hideous old hag, who scuttled around the room, leering and cackling to herself. Accounts were varied and uncertain. William suspected that Patrick Farrell knew something about the mysterious spirit and also a little of the history of the room itself. Whatever he knew, the lame man wasn't saying.

William's mind drifted over other topics. There was to be a grand party at Kilscosgriff, with guests coming from all over Ireland and England. Despite its enormous size, the castle would be absolutely full of visitors who would all need somewhere to sleep. William, who had recently returned from overseas, was used to 'roughing it' as an officer on active service in the army, and had volunteered to give up his newly

refurbished bedroom. It had slowly dawned on him, however, that there was now only one room left in the castle to
accommodate him — the celebrated Haunted Room. Despite
his apparent skepticism, the prospect unsettled him. He had
hoped that Patrick would reassure him, but the old man's
words had only disturbed him more.

As time passed, William's foreboding increased. Although
he was determined not to show it, the thought of spending a
night in the Haunted Room filled him with dread. Patrick
Farrell, limping around on his duties, gave him some
strange, dark glances and soon the young officer began to
wonder if he'd been wise to agree to the adventure at all.

It was the evening of the party and the old castle was full
to bursting. Wine and conversation flowed liberally, pushing all thoughts of the Haunted Room out of William's
mind. However, as the night wore on, several of the guests
joked about the Haunted Room. William took this to mean
that the boisterous party guests would conspire to play a
trick on him.

More unsettling was the odd behaviour of old Patrick Farrell. As he went about his duties, William could have sworn
the old man had made some sort of gesture in his direction,
involving the first and last fingers of his right hand. William
knew this sign. It was an ancient sign of protection, used by
the early Irish to ward off evil. The fact that Patrick Farrell
felt William needed such protection did nothing to allay the
young army officer's fears.

At the end of the evening, old Patrick followed William into one of the downstairs rooms.

'I would ask ye, Master William, t'think again about sleeping in yon room,' the old servant said in a low voice. William's brows knitted in a frown. Maybe Patrick was finally going to tell him about the room?

'Tell me, Patrick, tell me what you know.'

But the old man just looked away.

'I only know that there's them about here this very night that can stir up oul' echoes,' he replied, turning away. 'Them that you should have no business with. Them that'll cause trouble for you and yours for generations t'come – if you let them. That dark room'll draw ye all together. For your own good an' the good o' them that come after you, I ask you not to sleep there this night!'

William's frown deepened at the old servant's ramblings.

'Who is it? Is it somebody amongst the guests here tonight? Does someone mean me harm?' he enquired, but Patrick Farrell merely limped out of the room without further comment.

William wanted to run after him, to make him explain his queer warning, but instead he returned slowly to the merriment in the main hall.

Later that night, when all the guests were either asleep or gone home, William made his way along the corridor that led up to the Haunted Room. He checked under his coat, feeling the reassuring butts of two pistols there. They were his old army weapons. If anyone decided to play a nasty trick on him this night, he wasn't the only one who would get a fright!

The dark corridor led past heavy and gaudily framed portraits to a small flight of steps. These led up and around a corner, beneath an ornamental archway, and into another corridor. This was lit only by a single guttering candle in a wall bracket, making it so gloomy that William could hardly see his hand in front of him. On a low card-table against the wall, a small, nodding, porcelain Buddha moved its head in the draught, making William jump. He patted his pistols again for reassurance. The corridor ended abruptly in a doorway. William paused, then opened the door.

He blinked in surprise. As haunted chambers went, this room wasn't bad. In fact, it was actually rather pleasant. It was large and airy, and hung with beautiful tapestries. A number of candles, set in convenient niches, threw out a mellow and welcoming light. There was a huge, soft-looking four-poster bed, a washstand, several comfortable chairs, a bookcase and a roaring fire in the large fireplace — a maid must have set a good fire while it was still light. As a result, the Haunted Room was warm and dry. Indeed, it was so inviting that William thought that the stories that he'd heard about it across the years must have been myth.

And yet, as he sat in one of the fireside chairs, William remembered the strange looks and the ancient gesture he'd seen Patrick Farrell make. He remembered too the old man's warning — that there was someone in the castle who might cause torment to his own family for generations to come. What on earth did that mean?

As the candles burned down and the shadows lengthened along the panelled walls, Willliam began to sense a subtle chill in the room. The fire's comforting crackling and spluttering now seemed to take on a sinister and threatening air. He'd laid the pistols on a table by the side of the bed and, occasionally, he felt his eyes stealing anxiously in their direction.

The shadows moving silently around the room seemed to meld and change. Was that the figure of a man with a dagger in his raised hand in the far corner, just beyond the friendly glow of the candle ...? No, it was just a curiously formed clot of darkness. Was that a hunched black shape watching him intently from out of the gloom ...? No, it was just the end of the bookcase, grotesquely distorted by the shadows. William looked towards the bell-pull beside the bed. The maids said that it sometimes rang down in the kitchen, sharply, as if somebody was calling for help, even though there was never anybody in the room. Why was that he wondered? And why would no servant enter here after sunset?

The fire burned low and William threw a few more lumps of coal on it, making it spark and flare once more. This sort of thinking was getting him nowhere, he reasoned — it was only putting him on edge. He was very tired after the party and he had to get some sleep. But what was that? A noise outside his door? It sounded very like a woman's voice, speaking low. Getting up, William walked across to the chamber door and looked out.

There was nobody outside, only the porcelain Buddha nodding in the draught from the open door. But he was almost sure that he'd heard somebody speaking softly in the corridor. Behind him, one of the candles flickered and threatened to go out, throwing strange shadows across he room. The flame strengthened once more and the mellow light returned.

Wearily, William turned back into the room and prepared himself for bed. As he climbed between the sheets and watched the fire burn down, he cast an eye at the pistols on the bedside table and prayed that he wouldn't have to use them, even to scare somebody. He left one candle burning and, by its light, he could at least see part of the room. Despite his apprehension, the bed was comfortable and he could feel himself becoming drowsy.

'There's them about here this very night that can stir up oul' echoes.' Old Patrick Farrell's strange warning reverberated in the far corners of William's mind. Gradually, he drifted into a light and uneasy doze.

It must have been in the early hours of the morning when William was awoken by a faint sound, like the scratching of a mouse behind the wainscoting. Still half-asleep, he turned in the bed with a faint groan — and then sat bolt-upright in shock. The door to the bedroom was open.

A chill crept all along his body. Lying down and pulling the bedclothes tightly round him, he stared at the doorway with a fascinated terror. From beyond came a faint and murky light, which was moving. As he continued to watch, a young woman entered the room, wearing a white nightdress and carrying a lit candle. William pretended to be asleep but continued to watch through half-closed eyelids as the figure in white made her way slowly over to the bedside table and set her candle down. To William's surprise, she then climbed into bed beside him and extinguished the light. As she did so, William caught sight of an enormous sparkling ring on the middle finger of her right hand.

Under the bedclothes, the woman lay very still, as if she were asleep. William reached out and touched her gently on the shoulder. She was as warm and solid as himself. Who was she and what was she doing here? Maybe, William thought, she was one of the other guests, who had strayed from her own room and, being unfamiliar with the castle, had come into his by accident. Or maybe she was a sleepwalker and didn't know what she was doing? Or maybe it was a trick designed to cause him embarrassment? William didn't know what to think.

Not wishing to cause the lady any distress, William remained quiet and said nothing. He noticed that her right hand — the one upon which the great ring sparkled — was resting on the coverlet. Reaching across, he very slowly removed the gem from her finger and placed it on his own. If this were a trick, at least he'd have evidence of it in the morning.

After a short time in this attitude, the woman rose again, relit her candle and left the room as quietly as she'd come.

William lay awake for some time after, vainly trying to make sense of it all. For some reason, old Patrick Farrell's warning played at the back of his mind — was it somehow linked to the incident? Eventually, a dark and troubled sleep overcame him and he dozed until morning.

Not surprisingly after his disturbed night, William was one of the last into the breakfast room where all the guests were assembled. Looking at the many faces around the tables, he saw no trace of his nocturnal visitor. Seated at his own breakfast, he toyed with the peculiar ring, turning it round and round his finger in an absent manner.

'Where did you get that ring?' asked a sharp voice behind him. Turning, William found himself looking into the face of the young lady he'd seen in his room the night before. Like himself, she'd come down late to breakfast and was now standing looking fixedly at the jewellery on his finger. 'I recognise it as mine, for it's a family heirloom with no other like it,' the young lady went on, 'And I can't think how you came by it except that you entered my bedroom and stole it!'

'Indeed, I did not,' retorted William, blushing hotly at the insinuation. 'It was you who came into my room — and even into my bed — and it was then that I took the ring from your pretty hand.'

The young woman, whose name turned out to be Gertrude St. Ledger, looked at William in utter astonishment. She swore hadn't left her room all night. With further conversation, the two found that, not only was Gertrude's bedroom in a completely different part of the castle to the Haunted Room, but Gertrude's maid was sharing it. There was no way that Gertrude could have wandered out of the room and so far afield in her sleep without waking her. Yet there was the ring on William's finger.

Apart from discussing the inexplicable mystery of the ring, Gertrude and William were sensing something else — a strong and mutual attraction. The two of them continued talking long after the other guests had vacated the breakfast room. They seemed to have so much in common. William could feel himself drowning in Gertrude's beautiful eyes ...

'Take the ring back,' blurted William, several hours later. 'And while you're at it ... I beg you, Gertrude, please — take me with it!'

It was a most peculiar, impulsive proposal. William couldn't really say why he felt compelled to make it, except there was something about the girl that drew and fascinated him. Obviously she was very attractive, but there was more. Although they had shared the briefest acquaintance, William felt that he'd known Gertrude for a long, long time. And after all, he smirked to himself, they had shared a bed, albeit briefly ...

Gertrude St. Ledger, like William himself, came from an old family, long established in Ireland. Indeed, she was the sister of the first Viscount Doneraille and a young woman of considerable means. To William's delight, she immediately agreed to his odd proposal, and soon preparations were being finalised for their marriage.

Meanwhile, William noticed a distinct unease about old Patrick Farrell. The crippled servant made it clear he didn't approve of the wedding, although whom the young master married was none of his business. He kept giving the couple dark looks when he passed them, and more than once William saw him repeat the strange protective gesture he'd first made on the night of the party. However, it was a small blight on an otherwise happy existence. The wedding went ahead as planned, and William's new wife continued to wear with pride the ancient ring that had brought them so strangely together.

One day, William went down the corridor full of paintings that led to the Haunted Room. As a married man he was now in need of money, and though he'd never actually paid much attention to the portraits of his ancestors, he was now wondering what they were worth. As he walked, he happened to glance up at one of the dusty pictures that hung close to the steps to the room.

It was of a woman standing against dark background with her right hand clasped to her bosom. But what took William's attention as he passed, was the startling resemblance the face in the portrait bore to the face of William's own wife! He looked at the picture more closely and as he did so, his eyes widened in astonishment, for on the third finger of the right hand was the same ring his wife wore.

That evening, an intrigued William told Gertrude about the painting, and the next day he took her down to the dim corridor to have a look at it. She could offer no explanation as to the identity of the woman in the portrait or why she wore the St. Ledger family ring. Enquiries were made in both families but nobody knew anything about it. The painting had been hanging there for years and the identity of its subject had long been forgotten.

William tried one more line of enquiry. He asked Patrick Farrell about the lady in the portrait.

'I couldn't rightly tell who it is, but I did hear something years ago,' the old man finally admitted. 'They say that yon picture's of a woman that was "associated" with your family a long time ago — about 1703 or thereabouts. She had a connection with an ancestor of yours who had the same name as yourself — William Langford — and he was in the army as well. They say she was murdered in this very castle, and has a restless spirit wandering.' Farrell looked at William with a beady stare. 'How do you know that spirit's not attached to that oul' ring that your wife's so fond of?'

'That's preposterous old superstition, Patrick, and you should know better,' protested William.

'Ah, you should never have married her, Master William. She has stirred up oul' echoes, old memories of things that should've been left to the past.' And he looked directly at the young man with a queer, moody stare. 'Don't ask me anything else about it if you're not going to believe me — I wouldn't speak of it anyway.'

William was certain that the old man knew more than he was letting on. A murder or a terrible crime, was that the poor woman's history? And how was it that she looked so much like his own dear Gertrude? However, nothing more about the portrait or the murder could be discovered, nor was anything more found out about Gertrude's ring. William decided to let the matter rest.

Tragically, William's marriage lasted only five years. Gertrude had never been very strong and when influenza swept through Limerick, it brought her to the point of death. A frantic and desperate William called in the best physicians he could afford, but they could do nothing. At times Gertrude seemed to rally and his hopes rose, only to sink again when she would slide back into delirium. It gradually became apparent that she was gently slipping away. Eventually, weak and feverish, she called her distraught husband to her.

'I'm not long for this world, William dear,' she told him. 'But I make you one last promise. Your family has always been good to me, as have you, my dear, and I promise faithfully to watch over the Langford line. When death is poised to strike, William, I will warn those living here at the castle. By this small mercy, maybe I will not feel I am so alone ...' As she spoke, Gertrude sobbed and slid the ring from her finger. She gave it to William. 'Here, take my ring, dearest. As long as it remains in your family, I'll keep my promise!'

Although a strong man, tears streamed down William's face.

'Don't cry, William,' said Gertrude, 'My bond with you and yours will never die. I'll always be here, waiting in the shadows of Kilcosgriff ...'

The following day, a maid was cleaning in the Haunted Room and stepped out momentarily to fetch something. Suddenly the door to the chamber banged shut behind her, although there was no draught. When she tried to get back into the room, the door refused to open — as though a great weight had been pushed against it. The maid called for help from a number of sturdy footmen. They all tried, and couldn't open it either. The door remained immovable for about an hour, when it suddenly sprang open of its own accord. When the servants looked round, they realized that the portrait of the strange woman had fallen from the wall in the shadowy corridor and shattered. A piece of glass had pierced the canvas and it was destroyed beyond repair. At the same moment another servant came running to tell the news that Gertrude St. Ledger was dead.

Thus was born the legend of the White Lady of Kilcosgriff Castle, who followed the Coplan-Langfords and those associated with them for many years afterwards.

'A dark shadow has fallen across this castle,' intoned old Patrick Farrell. 'Master William's marriage stirred up old things that were better left sleeping.' But that was all that he would say on the subject. 'There'll be no good come of all this,' he would mutter darkly.

In a sense, the lame servant was correct, for the first death to be heralded by the appearance of the spectre was his own. As old Farrell lay on his deathbed, a maid was clearing some furniture along a corridor near the Haunted Room. Looking up, she saw a woman dressed in a long white gown, standing in the shadows at the foot of the stairs. The figure, the maid declared later, was about the same height and 'had the same way of standing and the same manner as Miss Gertrude ... and her in the clay.' Furthermore, when the figure raised her right hand, there on the third finger was the ring that Gertrude had always worn when alive. As the maid cried out, the strange lady turned, went up the stairs and round the corner towards the Haunted Room. The maid ran after the figure, only to witness it vanishing through the locked door. The girl then fainted and it was only much later that she heard that Patrick Farrell had died, at the very moment that she'd seen the spectre in the shadowy corridor.

When he heard the chilling tale, William Langford went into his study, opened a drawer in his bureau and took out his wife's ring. He sat for a long time looking at its curious carving and large glittering stone. All this time, it had been locked away in his study, so how had the so-called ghost come to be wearing it? Was this ring the work of Satan himself, he wondered? Its mystery had always been far beyond him – and he wanted rid of it. So he simply took the ring and hid it somewhere in the castle grounds – exactly where has never been discovered to this day.

For many years, the White Lady was not seen along the gloomy corridors of Kilcosgriff Castle. She didn't appear to tell of her husband William's death – or if she did, William never admitted it — and a number of the Langfords passed away without her warning.

Sixty years later, a Richard Langford inherited the castle. One night, he was retiring to bed when he heard an eerie sound. A large black setter dog, one of his own hounds, had got up onto the pier-gate and was howling most dismally. Pulling on a robe over his nightgown, Richard went outside to see if he could entice the animal down. It was a clear winter night with a frosty moon, big and bright, and he could see the entire outside of the castle just as clearly as if it were day. Richard tried to call the dog down but it gazed back at him with huge and mournful eyes and continued to howl.

Slowly, Richard realized that the animal wasn't really looking at him but at something beyond him. He turned. Standing on the other side of the courtyard and in the shadows of a building was a woman, dressed in a white gown of filmy material. She appeared to be watching keenly his ineffective attempts to bring the dog down. As he began to speak to her, she raised her right hand in a warning manner and the moonlight sparkled on the stone of a great ring. As he watched, astonished and a little uneasy, the woman crossed the yard and, with a final look backwards, vanished into the open door of a stable. Curious, Richard rushed across the yard and followed her in. The stable was in darkness, with nothing there except a solitary horse. Lighting the lantern hanging inside the door, Richard looked around him.

'Hello?' he called. 'Is there anybody there?'

At first there was no answer save for the renewed howling of the dog outside. Then Richard heard a woman's sigh from deep within the stable, but though he looked, he found no one. Baffled, he returned to bed. The dog kept howling all night. In the morning, Richard received news that his father had died the night before in Milltown Malbay.

It was Richard Langford's daughter, who was then a single lady of mature years, who next saw the phantom. Late one evening, Miss Langford was sitting in the dining room at Kilcosgriff reading a letter when she was disturbed by a strange and unearthly wailing sound coming from the gardens outside. Going over to the window, she looked out but could see nothing in the gathering dark. The sound, however, rose in intensity. Nervously, Miss Langford called her brother from another room, but as soon as he entered, the sound stopped. Laughing, Miss Langford's brother dismissed her as fanciful — 'No more than a dog or some sort of animal out in the garden' — and went back to his own room.

As soon as he'd left, the sound recommenced. Looking out again, the frightened woman saw a figure in white — unmistakably that of a lady — pass along a garden path known as the Lovers' Walk. Though it was dark, she could make out the shape, before it disappeared into a clump of laurels. Miss Langford hurried outside to the spot — but found no-one there. That same night, her Langford grandmother died.

Across the years, several attempts were made to find the ring that William Langford had hidden somewhere in the grounds of Kilcosgriff Castle. Even the Haunted Room was thoroughly searched from top to bottom, but nothing was ever discovered. Perhaps, said local folk, the ring had returned to the Devil whence it came.

There were also attempts to find out exactly who the strange phantom in white might be — was it Gertrude St. Ledger or was it an earlier spectre, perhaps of the woman in the portrait? Again, there was no definitive answer. The only tantalizing clue was an old story that refused to die down of an unnamed lady who had been married to the original William Langford in 1703 — and to whom something terrible but unspecified had happened at Kilcosgriff Castle.

* * *

In 1914, the White Lady changed her location, though she was still attached to the Coplan-Langfords. Mr. Crawford Langford, who had been in failing health for some time, chose to visit his cousin, a Major Langford D.S.O., at The Abbey, Rathkeale. For several days after his arrival, Mr Langford's health seemed to improve, but then illness took hold of him again and he grew worse. Two nurses were brought in to look after him and this account by one of them tells of an encounter with the White Lady.

'On a February evening in 1914, I was sitting in Mr Crawford's bedroom at around five o'clock. He'd been very ill during the day but he'd slipped into a sound sleep and I suppose that I was dozing a little bit myself. The other nurse looked in but I said to her, "You go down and have tea and I'll wait here with Mr. Crawford." I was frightened of him waking and taking a turn, you see. After she'd gone, I dozed a little more. I was seated with my back towards the fireplace, just opposite the sick man's bed and there was a pleasant and drowsy heat in the room. I was disturbed out of my drowsing by the sound of the door opening very gently. Thinking that it was the other nurse, I struggled to open my eyes. "You weren't long," I said. "You should have taken a bit longer for I could've managed. He's sleeping like a baby anyhow." There was no answer, so I opened my eyes more fully. I wasn't alone in the room. A tall lady dressed all in white was crossing towards the invalid's bed. She walked, or should I say glided, over the floor, her eyes fixed on the sick man and with a look of intense anguish on her face. Mr. Crawford moaned and tossed at her approach and I opened my mouth to say something, but no words would come.

'Reaching the bed, she bent over Mr. Crawford and appeared to lay her hand on his forehead. It was then that I saw a great, sparkling, ugly-looking old ring on the third finger of her right hand. Almost at once, Mr. Crawford appeared to ease and returned to his sound sleep once more. The woman turned to me as if to speak but instead gave a dazzling smile and vanished. I was alone in the room again with Mr. Crawford sleeping quietly. But even then, I could hear the gasps in his breath. Moments later, the other nurse came

in to relieve me and I told her what had happened — told her
that I might have seen a ghost, but she wouldn't believe me.
"No such things as ghosts," she said rather abruptly, "You've
had no more than a dream." And for a day or so I believed
that's all it had been. But, from that very night, Mr. Crawford's condition got steadily worse, though he'd been making
a kind of recovery earlier. Within six days he was dead. Later,
I heard about Kilcosgriff Castle and about the White Lady
that follows the Langfords and I knew what I'd seen. I can see
her yet, with that great old ring shining from her finger as she
touched his forehead ...'

* * *

The last sighting of the White Lady comes from Dublin. It
appears that a certain Miss Langford took a house around
Merrion Square, sometime in the mid-1920s. During her
stay there, she had cared for her sister, who was recovering
from surgery and who was very weak. She was, however,
expected to make a good recovery provided she took things
easy.

Late one night, Miss Langford was awakened from a sound
sleep by a noise in the street outside her window. Alarmed,
she went over to see the cause of the curious commotion,
which sounded like a cross between a woman crying and a dog
howling. Looking down from her bedroom window she saw,
by the light of a street gas lamp, a woman dressed in white

standing directly underneath and looking up at the house. The woman appeared to be beckoning and Miss Langford was able to glimpse the inevitable flash of her ring in the wan streetlight. As Miss Langford stood transfixed, she heard the convalescent cough in the next room and instinctively turned her head in the direction of the sound. When she turned back, the street was empty. There's little need to relate that her sister's condition suddenly took a turn for the worse that night and that within two or three days she was dead.

So who was the White Lady and what was the significance of her ancient ring? Many of the Langford family still believe that she was the ghost of Gertrude St. Ledger. To this day, there is no satisfactory explanation for either. The strange story, together with Kilcosgriff Castle and its Haunted Room, have long passed into folk memory — but perhaps, even today, the shade still follows the Langfords, warning of doom and death. Who knows what still may lurk in the spectral shadows?

The House on the Hill of Weeping

In many instances, the reputation of a 'haunted house' depends on our own response to the nature of the building itself and its environment. Such a response is usually made on a primitive emotional level. An eerie setting, bleak weather conditions or a sinister history may conspire to create in us feelings of fear, awe or horror. Sometimes an atmosphere can be so strong that researchers have argued that it has somehow imprinted on the very fabric of the bricks and mortar of, say, an old house, to be experienced again in future years by those sensitive enough to pick up the vibrations. In this way, goes the theory, powerful emotions, such as hatred, anxiety or love, are simply replayed time and again as easily as a CD or video recording.

One of the most powerful emotions of all, of course, is love. The ghostly re-emergence of a passionate love that has somehow defeated death and is doomed to well up again sporadically across the centuries is a common feature of ghost lore. Thus, we get lovelorn maidens and heroes wandering the corridors, rooms and passageways of many an old house, ceaselessly searching for lost loves or seeking to recapture past romances. Perhaps it is the power of our own emotional response to their love stories that allows us to see them.

But if pure and unsullied love is strong enough to leave its imprint behind, then perhaps its poor relation, lust, may also leave its dark mark. There are a number of tales featuring lustful ghosts that haunt certain buildings, obsessively seeking the object of their unsatisfied desire. A particularly horrible example of such a spirit is said to be found at Thirlstane Castle in Berwickshire, Scotland. Here, the lecherous ghost of John Maitland, Duke of Lauderdale, close friend of King Charles II and Secretary of State for Scotland, pursues the screaming wraiths of his victims along the echoing corridors of his former mansion. In life, Maitland was a rapist and a bully. His second wife, the notorious Elizabeth Murray, Countess of Dysart, was rumoured to be a lesbian – more seriously, she was suspected of having murdered her first husband. Throughout their marriage, Maitland not only conducted a number of extra-marital affairs, but also forced his loathsome attentions on several serving women, who had no recourse against him. His lustful phantom still haunts his one-time home and the nearby St. Mary's Church, where he is interred in the family vault. Old people in the area still go in fear of the raging spectre of Thirlstane and of the attendant shades of those whom he so roughly violated.

Ireland too, has its share of such sites. The most famous of them lies not far from the Hill of Tara in County Meath. Here again, lust and violation play a significant part in the origins of the ghost story, echoes of which have found their way down to the present century. The brutality and brooding violence of the history of the place will not easily be laid to rest ...

Close by the Hill of Tara, the ancient and atmospheric seat of the High Kings of Ireland, is another hill known as Cnoc Ghuil, or the Hill of Weeping. There are many stories as to how it came by its name. It may have been an ancient battlefield where women wept over the bodies of their fallen husbands. It may have been a place of punishment where prisoners were sent to a horrible death by the ancient kings of Tara. Whatever the origins of its name, by the early medieval period the hill had already acquired a mysterious, somewhat sinister, reputation. In spite of this and of its proximity to the ancient and mystical Tara, a twelfth-century Norman knight known as Adam de Feipo built a fortress on its southern slope. Skyrne Castle was its name.

Across the succeeding centuries, Skyrne Castle changed hands several times, gradually sliding into ruin and neglect. A local legend sprang up claiming that it was haunted by the figure of a tall, heavily cloaked man, walking with a hound. The ghost of a nun was also seen near the crumbling tower.

Even when the present house was built around the old central tower, and beautiful and extensive grounds were laid out around it, the hauntings continued. The most prominent phantom is that of a screaming woman in white. Her ghastly shrieks are said to echo around the castle and its grounds as she is pursued by a monstrously dark and menacing shadow. Who is this strange phantom and why does she scream? And what is the terrible shadow that pursues her? The origins of her awful story may lie in a violent incident that took place in the early eighteenth century.

At this time, Skyrne Castle was in the hands of an old English family, the Casways. The master of the house, Sir Bromley Casway, was a miserly, self-centred, malicious old man who suffered greatly from gout and who was largely confined to a wicker wheelchair. One day, news reached Sir Bromley that a tragic accident had befallen a distant relation and his wife — the Palmerstons. Both had been killed while holidaying abroad, leaving their eighteen-year-old daughter, Lilith. As Lilith's only surviving relative, Sir Bromley had been appointed her guardian.

The old man received this news with mixed emotions. The girl would obviously have to come and live with him. On the one hand, she would be another mouth to feed, but on the other, the old man needed somebody to look after him since he was too mean to pay any servants. He could use Lilith Palmerston as an unpaid drudge, at his beck and call. Sir Bromley decided she would be welcomed.

So it was that Lilith Palmerston came to Skyrne Castle under the direct wardship of Sir Bromley Casway. In fact, she was very glad to be there, for her parents' death had left her without a penny or a roof over her head. Her father had died owing large amounts of money, and his entire estate was now in the hands of his creditors. Lilith had nothing. Therefore, she depended on Sir Bromley's generosity, protection and forbearance.

Lilith quickly learned that her vulnerable position meant she had to endure the indignities that the old man heaped upon her. He was not physically violent towards her — he was far too frail for that — but he treated her like the lowest of the servants, making her answer to his every whim and cursing her viciously when she was slow or made a mistake. She had to prepare his meals, fix his bath, push him about in his chair, write his letters and, as the old blackguard's eyesight was failing, she had to read to him each evening. His preferred reading material concerned the exotic Far East or darkest Africa, and many of his books described the strange and mysterious rituals that were practiced there. These, along with the customs of the natives of certain South Sea Islands, seemed to fascinate the ancient devil and he never lost an opportunity to draw her attention to a particularly gory or frightening portion of the text.

'Do you believe in ghosts, child?' Sir Bromley would ask in his high and querulous old man's voice. When Lilith answered that she didn't really know, he would cackle. 'They say that this castle is greatly haunted,' he would remind her. 'It's said that Adam de Feipo, the Norman lord that built it, did so on the site of a very ancient graveyard. The ghosts from that place are supposed to prowl the passageways of Skyrne looking for tender young flesh, like the Hottentots in those far-off countries. Horrible to look upon they are, and their appetites are insatiable!' And he would pause to watch for her reaction, which was usually one of fear. 'But you don't believe those old stories, do you, Lilith?' He would assume an air of unruffled piety. 'Trust in the Lord, child, and no dreadful harm will come to you. At least, that's what we hope!' And he would laugh horribly.

Although Lilith didn't really believe in spirits, she still felt that the old place was oppressive and eerie. Her ancient relative's attitude didn't help. She knew that when she'd gone to bed, he went about the lower floors in his wheelchair as though he was looking for something along the corridors. Late at night, she could hear the distant squeak of the wheels as he went through the darkened house. She suspected him of trying to frighten her with his strange goings-on. Well, if that was what he was up to, he was succeeding — she hadn't slept properly since she'd arrived. Lilith grew to loathe and despise her elderly guardian but she had to put up with him. If she left, where could she go? Who else would take her in?

Almost a year after she'd come to Skyrne, Lilith gained a respite from the old man. She was sent away to a fashionable school in Dublin, where she blossomed into a beautiful young woman who was well noticed on the City's society circuit. She thoroughly enjoyed her time in Dublin, doing the rounds of the society balls and parties and drawing the admiration of many young men. For a while, Skyrne Castle and her hateful guardian were little more than memories.

Meanwhile, back in County Meath, Sir Bromley had taken a minor 'turn'. He demanded that Lilith come back to look after him. The selfish old man gave the girl herself scant thought — he needed full-time nursing and Lilith would have to step in. Reluctantly, she returned to Skyrne and resumed her former duties. There seemed very little wrong with the ancient rogue, but he inflicted the same drudgery on her as before.

From time to time, Sir Bromley attempted to terrify Lilith with hints about ghosts. 'D'you think this place is haunted?' he would ask suddenly. 'I've heard that it was built on a druid site, 4,000 years old, and that there's a great man that walks around the castle with a long cloak on him. The ghost of an old druid maybe? What d'you think, girl? There's supposed to be a big hellhound with glowing eyes that walks with him. Do you think that they'd do you harm if you met them one night?' And he would laugh unpleasantly, showing rotting teeth. 'Maybe not, if you put your trust in the Church!'

It was a melancholy and lonely existence. Much of the time, she paid her guardian's words no heed. There were nights, however, as the wind blew mournfully about the towers and buttresses of Skyrne, that she felt a twinge of apprehension. There were noises about the house, which may have been Sir Bromley moving about in his wheelchair through the darkened corridors. Sometimes Lilith thought that she heard voices calling to her on the night wind — calling her to come away and leave the gloomy castle behind.

Occasionally, Sir Bromley would send Lilith down to the cellars of Skyrne to fetch a bottle of wine to drink with dinner. The wine cellar was dank and gloomy, and often filled with the scratching of rats or mice. Lilith hated the place — it was the part of the castle in which she felt most vulnerable. When forced to go there, she told herself that she was being silly, and tried to pushed her fears to the back of her mind.

One problem, though, refused to go away — but it wasn't anything to do with the supernatural. When she had been away in Dublin, Sir Bromley had taken up with a neighbouring squire named Phelim Sellars. Sellars was a huge, coarse man about middle age, with a quick temper and a foul tongue. He had taken over a nearby farm and his land bordered that of the Casways. He would often call at Skyrne, usually late in the evening, to play cards or have a smoke with the old man. He was a widower who lived alone, and initially Lilith had felt rather sorry for him. She soon revised her opinion when she heard the stories concerning Sellars that were circulating in the district. Rumour had it that he'd treated his first wife — a young woman of about Lilith's age — extremely badly. She had eventually died in suspicious circumstances. The local gossips claimed that he'd beaten her to death in a fit of temper.

One evening Sellars called to play cards with Sir Bromley. Lilith opened the door to him. As soon as he saw her, an unhealthy and lascivious light flashed in Sellars' eyes. Lilith was certainly a beauty and had developed over her time in Dublin and now the brutal squire looked at her lustfully, desiring her with an awful intensity. As she brought him into the house, he refused to take his eyes off the way her body

moved. Not quite under his breath, he made coarse comments, which Lilith pretended not to hear as she guided him
to the great drawing room.

Sellars' visits became torture for Lilith. Most evenings, he
would call just after the evening meal was finished and he and
Sir Bromley would retire to the drawing room where they
would often play cards until the early hours. During these
visits, Lilith was treated very much like a servant by her guardian, having to fetch and carry for them both, answering the
old man's every call. And, of course, every time she entered
the room she'd be aware of Phelim Sellars' eyes on her, men-
tally undressing her as she attended to Sir Bromley's orders.

Several times Lilith tried to raise the subject of Sellars'
attitude and of how much she detested the squire's presence
at the castle, but Sir Bromley simply waved these objections
away with a motion of his palsied hand. He would not hear a
word spoken against his guest. So Sellars continued to make
her life a misery as, emboldened by his host's indifference, he
began to take more and more liberties with Lilith.

One evening as she was bending over the card table to pour
Sir Bromley a glass of sherry, the squire reached across and
put his hand under her skirts in a very over-familiar manner.
For once, Lilith showed her mettle.

'I would thank you to remove your hand, sir!' she said, her
face flushing. 'And I would further thank you not to make so
free with my guardian's hospitality. What you've done is a
breach of whatever good name you possess and is an affront to

me, to my guardian and to this house! I would ask you not to touch me again. If you do, I will ask Sir Bromley to have you thrown out!'

For a moment, Sellars looked at her stupidly as if he couldn't believe what he was hearing, then he burst into gusts of braying laughter.

'The girl has spirit, Sir Bromley,' he guffawed. 'I'll give you that. Forgive me, Lilith dear,' his words were oozing with lust and hypocrisy. 'I didn't mean to offend. It was only a prank, and I trust that both you and Sir Bromley will overlook my momentary lapse?' And he shot a glance towards the old man in his wheel-chair on the other side of the table. Sir Bromley looked up.

'There's nothing to apologise for, Phelim,' he answered. Turning to Lilith, he said sternly: 'It was only a bit of light-hearted horseplay — but you've taken upon yourself to openly criticise one of my guests without my permission and I won't tolerate that. You will apologise to the squire for your imper-tinence. Do not be so forward again.'

Stunned, Lilith stammered a half-hearted apology.

'Now,' said Sir Bromley, 'Fetch some brandy and we'll say no more about it. But remember Lilith, that although you are my ward, you are also a guest under my roof — and I will decide as to what are proper manners here. You'll be more polite to my visitors in future.'

The rebuke was like a green light to the loathsome squire. Whenever he was in the castle — which was often — he never lost an opportunity to grab at Lilith, or to push himself against her in the most revolting and suggestive manner. There was little that the girl could do, for Sir Bromley was dismissive of her complaints. Sellars, he told her, was one of the local gentry, whereas she was dependent upon the good-will of others.

Even when Lilith briefly left the confines of Skyrne to take a walk in its beautiful grounds, the awful squire would be seen lurking around the area where his own land merged with that of Sir Bromley. There seemed to be no escape from him.

Lilith pleaded with her guardian to send her back to Dublin where she'd been happy. Every time she asked, Sir Bromley refused. His health was failing almost on a daily basis, he said, and he needed her at Skyrne to look after him. Having no money of her own, Lilith couldn't simply flee the place of her own accord — she was little better than a prisoner in the old house. She was hanging onto the hope that she would get a fraction of Sir Bromley's vast fortune when he died but, although he complained constantly, he showed no sign of expiring. As time went on, he became ever more cantankerous and demanding.

'Soon I'll be gone, child,' he would moan. 'And who'll be left to mourn me or to look after Skyrne Castle? I've no children — nobody to leave the place to. But who would want it? It's so badly haunted. At night, I hear ghosts everywhere, moving about. Don't you hear them too, Lilith?' Even in the middle of his endless complaining, he couldn't resist tormenting her.

'I hear nothing!' she would reply stiffly, and Sir Bromley would laugh wickedly, knowing that he'd unsettled her.

There were times, Lilith was ashamed to admit, when she wished that the old rogue would die — that she'd get up some morning to find him pale, stiff and cold in his bed. But every morning there he was, whining and complaining, worse than before.

If Sir Bromley annoyed her, Phelim Sellars frightened her. She did her best to avoid him, but he was always appearing unexpectedly, leering at her. Every time he caught her alone, he roughly tried to force his attentions on her. He seemed to grow coarser in his ways, making vile suggestions to her when they met that bordered on the obscene. He was drinking heavily, and the stink of him made Lilith's stomach turn.

Her life at Skyrne was having an effect upon Lilith. When she'd returned from Dublin she'd certainly been a beauty, but now her life of drudgery in the castle was taking its toll. Her looks began to fade and her youthful vivacity began to drain away. She'd become a near-recluse behind the old castle's sombre walls, and now took on some of the drabness that characterised the building itself.

This gradual loss of beauty and spirits didn't seem to discourage Phelim Sellars. His obsessive interest in her increased as she repelled his advances. She was appalled by the violence of his lust — and her fear of him grew as time went on. She pleaded with Sir Bromley to send her back to Dublin.

He always refused. Once she was gone, he said, he would have to pay a servant to look after him — and he wasn't going to part with a penny if he could help it, not when he had an inexpensive drudge already in place. Lilith spent more and more time in her room and often cried herself to sleep.

One summer's afternoon, a drunken Sellars called at Skyrne on the pretence of seeing Sir Bromley, but the owner of the castle was asleep and unable to receive him. Lilith dismissed Sellars and told him to go home. Closing the castle's main door on him, she went out into the garden to finish some work that she'd been doing there. Sellars, however, wouldn't be so easily dismissed. Creeping silently around the side of the castle, he followed Lilith into the garden. As the defenceless girl bent down over a flowerbed, Sellars leapt on her from behind.

Desperately, Lilith struggled to fight him off but, even in a drunken state, Sellars was stronger than she. His weight bore down on her as he stared at her, eyes red with drink and a ferocious lust. Lilith felt her dress tearing open at the front. With one desperate effort, she pushed him off her, broke free from his grabbing hands, and ran, screaming loudly, into the nearby woods. By now, some of the few servants that Sir Bromley still kept were coming. Fearing that he would be caught and held to account, Sellars ran off before he was seen.

In utter desperation after this attack, Lilith once again approached Sir Bromley. She told him what had occurred and begged to be sent back to Dublin. This time Sir Bromley didn't completely dismiss the suggestion and promised he'd think about it. His own doctor had expressed concerns about the health of the old man's ward. Besides, despite their supposed friendship, Sir Bromley himself thought that the squire had overstepped the mark. Sellars' visits to Skyrne became fewer — for which Lilith was more than grateful — but he still hung about the edges of Sir Bromley's lands, waiting for his chance.

In the end, Sir Bromley agreed to let Lilith go to Dublin for one year. Sellars had been making a nuisance of himself and perhaps it was best if Lilith was out of his way for a time. Overjoyed, Lilith began to make preparations for her departure.

Some of the servants who worked for Sir Bromley also worked for the squire from time to time, and it was from them that he received news of Lilith's plans. It sent him into a foul, dark spiral of aggression that was worsened by his heavy drinking. The night before Lilith's departure, he drunkenly mounted a grey horse and rode over to Skyrne Castle. As he galloped, he worked himself into a fury. He would soon teach Lilith a lesson — she wasn't going anywhere.

At the castle, Sellars pounded on the door and demanded entry. One of the servants let him in, but told him that Sir Bromley had retired to bed, as had Miss Lilith. Pushing the servant aside, Sellars stormed up the main staircase towards Lilith's room.

Lilith was packing, but the commotion in the hallway below drew her out into the hallway. Startled, she saw Sellars, his face twisted in anger, racing up the stairs.

'How dare you? How dare you come here and force your way in at this time of night!' Lilith's voice was strong though her heart was fluttering. 'Sir Bromley's asleep and cannot be disturbed. I've no wish to see you, so there's nothing for you here. Leave now — and don't return unless you're sent for!'

They were brave words and Sellars seemed taken aback for a moment. Then his face broke into a sly smile.

'So you think that you're leaving?' he asked. 'You think that you can run away to Dublin in order to get away from — one that wants you? Let me assure you, my lady, that you'll never leave Skyrne Castle without my blessing!'

His tone stung Lilith to fury.

'Be quiet, you cur!' she shouted. 'By what right do you come here, issuing threats? Get out of my sight, like the base blackguard you are, before Sir Bromley wakes and instructs his men to have you out into the gutter where you belong!'

Sellars' beady red eyes hardened.

'You think you can flirt and toss your head and then just walk away?' he growled.

'You know that I have never given you an ounce of encouragement, Phelim Sellars!' Lilith spat. 'You're nothing but a drunk and a worm and I've only ever felt disgust for you. Now get out of here before I fetch Sir Bromley to put the dogs on you!'

Sellars looked at Lilith stupidly for a moment. Then a look of pure contempt appeared in his eyes.

'What gives a low-born whore like you the right to spurn me?' he roared. 'You can sneer at me all you like – but I swear I'll have you before I'm finished!'

With that, Sellars pushed Lilith back towards her bedroom. 'We're going to have a little fun before you leave ...'

Lilith tried to scream for help, but Sellars clamped his hand over her mouth. Pushing her down on the bedroom door, he forced her knees apart and climbed on top of her. Lilith punched and clawed at his face but to little effect. Sellars was now so crazed with lust that nothing could deter him.

Lilith's flailing hand found a heavy figurine on a low table. Grabbing it, she tried to smash it over Sellars' head but the blow merely clipped the side of his face, drawing blood. Raising his hand to his bruised cheek, Sellars mad eyes grew more bloodshot and the veins stood out in his neck.

'You damned whore!' he screamed, grabbing Lilith by the throat. She struggled and fought for breath with an increasing desperation but his grip was too strong. With a howl of fury, Sellars squeezed her white throat. 'You'll never do this to me or any man ever again, you slut!' Lilith's eyes grew round and rolled back in her head. She flailed one more time, then fell back limply and was still.

It took Sellars a moment to realise that he'd killed her. With a cry of fright and despair, he scrambled to his feet, ran down the stairs and fled from Skyrne into the night.

Since Lilith's horrific murder had been witnessed by servants, Phelim Sellars was now a wanted man. A warrant was
quickly drawn up for his arrest and soldiers arrived at his
house to enforce it. They found it empty with not a trace of
the villainous squire to be found. A massive manhunt was
mobilised, with soldiers searching every deserted barn and
cottage in County Meath and further afield.

Sellars was caught boarding a ship for America from the
port of Dublin. His trial was swift and, being found guilty, he
was hanged in the gaol yard behind Clew Barracks. This
seemed to bring the awful affair to an end as far as the
authorities were concerned.

The effect of the murder upon Sir Bromley Casway was
severe. Not that the unfeeling old man mourned poor Lilith
greatly, but the fact was that a murder had been committed
under his roof. This lowered his status and added to the
already sinister reputation of Skyrne Castle. Already declin-
ing in health, Sir Bromley now deteriorated rapidly.

On certain nights, many local people declared that they
could hear the terrified phantom of Lilith Palmerston,
screaming loudly from the upper rooms of the old building
or from the garden and grounds around it, where Sellars had
first attacked her. There is no doubt that Sir Bromley heard
the dreadful sounds too as he sat alone in his wheelchair of a
night.

'D'you think that Skyrne Castle is haunted, child?' he'd once
taunted Lilith. Now he was certain that it was. Shortly after the

hanging of his one-time friend, Sir Bromley was found dead in his wheelchair, alone and with a look of terror on his livid face.

Skyrne Castle fell into the hands of distant Casway relatives. For years, the castle stood empty and untended, its silence shattered only by the screams of its terrified ghost — poor Lilith Palmerston pursued throughout eternity by the malignant phantom of Phelim Sellars. In the 1990s, the castle was bought by Elizabeth Hickey, a well-respected Irish historian. She professed herself at ease with the spirits of Skyrne, stating that her main interests lay in the area of historical fact rather than supernatural myth and legend. Yet those who have visited the castle in modern times claim that there's still a strange and oppressive atmosphere about the place, a kind of dread that hangs over the area like a shroud.

And so it remains today, a place apart and slightly withdrawn from the world. As crowds of tourists and sightseers rush past in order to view the ancient splendours of the nearby Hill of Tara, Skyrne Castle seems to be locked in the world of its own tragic past, a world of old sadnesses, violence and near-forgotten passions, where ghostly inhabitants shy away from our own bustling sphere of everyday reality.

Ardogina, the House of Madam Coghlan

I came on a great house in the middle of the night
Its open lighted doorway and its windows all alight
And all my friends were there and made me welcome too,
But I woke in an old ruin that the winds howled through ...

WB Yeats: 'The Curse of Cromwell'

Scattered all over Ireland are many old houses, which positively invite a supernatural reputation, either by their doomy appearance or by their troubled history. Many of them hark back to the days of the great families – both Irish and English – and are sometimes repositories of traditions better left unspoken. A number were destroyed or partly destroyed during the Irish Civil War in the 1920s, falling in a welter of fire and blood. Today, their overgrown shells serve as the only reminder of their former grandeur. Who can tell what has happened within such walls in times past?

Few of these houses are now inhabited – at least not by human beings – but memories linger of the people who lived there. There are ruined mansions like the bleak and windswept Tyrone House near Clarinbridge, County Galway, which is still haunted by the restless ghost of Christopher St. George. This young man disgraced his staunch Protestant family by committing the heinous crime of marrying a Catholic. There is also the intriguingly named Castle Strange near Athleague, County Roscommon, which was built for the L'Strange family. The house was built on a site where ancient Celtic rituals were held and eerie faces are often said to appear at the glassless windows. There is Timoney Park, close to Roscrea, County Tipperary. A phantom carriage is said to travel to this once-fine pile, carrying some of the long-dead Parker-Hutchinsons, the grand family who built and occupied the mansion.

These ruined houses are the last remnants of another age – a time of powerful landlords occupying a hostile land, whose history became entwined with that land and who were often touched by the ancient darkness of Celtic folklore and myth. They reflect triumph and tragedy, authority and repression – the struggle that is a part of Ireland's uneasy past. Is it any wonder, then, that many of them are believed to harbour ghosts?

'If that house isn't haunted then it bloody well should be!' Thus declared an old man as we viewed a distant ruin across his fields. Ardogina House is situated on lonely cliffs in County Waterford. Amongst its neglected rooms and abandoned, echoing halls, it's not hard to imagine the phantom grandeur of former days. Surely ghosts wander along the rubble-strewn corridors or dance in the weed-choked ballrooms where once the living held sway?

'You'll have heard of yonder black place?' The old man raised his walking stick and pointed into the distance, to where a single ivy-clad tower appeared over the trees.

I told him that I wasn't sure, and he snorted a little at my ignorance. Behind him, in the shadow of the cottage doorway, his equally ancient wife nodded silently. As I squinted in the late evening sunlight, he questioned me. How had I never heard of 'Ardo House', as it was called locally, and of the Coghlans who had once lived there? Surely I had heard of Madam Coghlan, for she was famous all across Ireland at one time! I confessed that I was a stranger to Waterford and the story of the Coghlans and their house had passed me by.

The old man shook his grizzled head. In this part of the country, ancient traditions were extremely important, he said. From the dark interior of the house, his wife continued to watch me quietly. Sometimes on dark nights, she said, they heard the Madam still singing, away across the fields. She always had a grand and musical voice. Her husband ignored these comments but I could not help noticing a tinge of apprehension in her voice. I noticed that her gaze rested uneasily on the distant tower.

Sensing a story, I turned once more to the old man who was leaning heavily on his stick. Maybe, I suggested, he could tell the story of Ardo and the Coghlans? Above, the seagulls wheeled and swooped, crying to each other as the light began to falter.

The old man drew himself up to his full height, obviously pleased to have his knowledge and experience recognised — even if only by a casual passer-by.

In fact, I'd not been completely honest with the old couple, for I had heard of Ardo before. While in Kilkenny one year, visiting some of the ruined houses of Ireland, I was told that a Madam Coghlan of Ardogina House had brought her husband's family to ruin. The story contained little detail and a lot of supposition, so I jumped at the chance to hear more from a local source. And I wasn't to be disappointed, for the old man was now pulling himself up and preparing to tell me the strange story of that distant, ruined mansion ...

* * *

Ardogina House had always had a queer, dark history about it. During the late 1600s, long before the Coghlans came, an older, smaller house stood on the site, with a good-sized estate for its day. This house was built by a family named Costen, who were the landowners around Ardmore.

The Costens were not a pleasant family — they continually fought amongst themselves and were generally considered a greedy, grasping clan. By the early 1700s, a young gentleman, whose name is sometimes given as Richard Costen, was the heir to the whole Ardo estate. Until he achieved legal age, however,

Ardogina was managed by a guardian — said to be an uncle — on his behalf. But when the young fellow was coming near the time when he could manage Ardo in his own right, the uncle was unwilling to let the property go. After all, he'd looked after it for years himself without anybody telling him what to do, and he looked on himself as the master there. Besides, he'd made a fortune from the letting of the lands round about. In short, he wanted the young heir out of the way.

So the uncle hatched a plan: he'd have Richard thrown into jail and he himself would stay on as master at Ardo. One night, he took some of his valuable silver spoons and plate, and hid them among Richards's things. Then he called in the local troops from Waterford Town and told them that he'd been robbed. It didn't take them long to find the items amongst Richard's possessions, branding him as the thief. The young man couldn't prove his innocence, so he did the only thing that he could do — he fled. Running to the stable yard, Richard leaped onto the back of the first horse that he came to — an untried grey that was saddled and bridled for exercising — and galloped off at full pelt.

This was the worst thing that he could have done, for it seemed to confirm his guilt. The troops immediately gave chase. All across the cliffs near Ardo, the hunt went on, with Richard just managing to keep ahead of the soldiers. At length, he came to a ravine, high above the sea.

Richard paused. If he could leap that, he was free and clear, but if he didn't, he'd be caught or killed. He was a plucky young fellow and decided to chance it. With the pounding of the troops' horses in his ears, Richard desperately urged on the spirited grey mare. She made an almighty leap, right across the ravine — and landed all four hooves on the other side.

But the worn saddle strap had broken. The saddle slipped and Richard Costen went with it. As the grey made solid ground, he fell off. His neck caught in the reins, as if he were in a noose. Dangling him over the ravine, Richard's legs kicked and twisted, frantically trying to gain a foothold — but, despite his struggle, the life eventually left him, just as surely as if he'd been hanged on a gallows for the crime he hadn't commited. Ever since, the site of the leap has been known as *Crooke an Heire*, or the Heir's Gallows, and there is a local tradition that when the wind from the sea is right, the blood-freezing screams of the dying Richard Costen can still be heard.

The Costen line at Ardo died out shortly afterwards. The place never really prospered following the stewardship of Richard's uncle. Within a generation it had passed out of the hands of the family. Its next owners were the Prendergasts, an old Norman family who had arrived in Ireland with the first English settlers.

The Prendergasts had plenty of money and status in Ireland. But soon after taking over Ardo, they ran into debt — possibly because they'd overspent on the estate. When the family fortunes hit rock bottom, old Sir Maurice Prendergast hanged himself from the banisters above the hall of Ardogina. A local story said that he had squandered all the family money, was 'in hock' to a host of Dublin moneylenders and hadn't any hope of paying them off. To him, it must have seemed that suicide was the only way out.

If Sir Maurice was a wastrel, the rest of his clan was dark and bloody. When Ardo was being refurbished years later, a skeleton was found under the dining-room floor. It was reputed to be that of a serving man whom one of the Prendergasts had murdered. The crime was laid at the door of Sir Francis Prendergast — a violent psychopath given to fierce tantrums, who was renowned for treating servants in the most appalling manner. The Prendergasts held Ardo for only a short time, and then the estate fell into the hands of the Coghlans.

Jeremiah Coghlan was a self-made man — a wealthy Protestant merchant from Waterford Town. He was decent enough and a hard worker, but he was weak and easily led. He liked fine things about him as much as any other rich man, but Jeremiah's main extravagance — and the cause of his undoing — was his wife.

Nobody around Ardmore ever knew her first name or where she'd come from. She was simply 'Madam Coghlan' or 'the Madam' when they spoke to or about her. Madam Coghlan was known for her ambition and her extravagance. She loved spending money and, no matter what he did, Jeremiah couldn't stop her. She was used to getting her way, and she wanted to turn Ardo into the grandest 'big house' in County Waterford — maybe even in the whole of Ireland — with herself as its doyenne. The Coghlans had four children — three girls and a boy — who were spoiled and kept in style. Two of the girls were great beauties, and one eventually married a French nobleman, the Duc de Castres. The two younger children were said to be 'weak-minded' and were hidden from view.

Building work at Ardo started with the aim of making it a stately mansion. Madam Coghlan used workmen from all over Ireland and England, paying them well for their time. The money came from Jeremiah Coghlan's business. At first, construction went according to plan. While the business was thriving, things were grand, but a slight unpleasantness in Waterford town between Jeremiah and some associates meant that the business — and the money — began to falter.

Even when this happened and money started growing scarce, Madam Coghlan continued with the extensions at Ardo, adding more and more to the building and turning it into her fantasy house, with all sorts of nooks and crannies and secret rooms where she could indulge herself. She never counted the cost of it, but the strain started to tell on Jeremiah Coghlan. He had fierce disagreements with his Catholic competitors and neighbours. Many of the people of Waterford boycotted him and soon he was facing financial ruin and bankruptcy. This situation made little impact on the Madam, who went on spending just as much as before. At last, her extravagance and the worry that came with it got the better of her husband. Exhausted, he took to his bed, and died shortly afterwards.

After Jeremiah's death, the Madam's spending increased rather than declined. Fine brocades were brought from overseas, furniture made from expensive woods, wonderful tailored clothes. She played up the part of an extremely wealthy widow — but everyone wondered how she managed to afford such luxuries. At the time of his death, Jeremiah's fortune hadn't been great and, now that Ardo was finished, it was an expensive house to maintain. Yet Madam took on even more servants and continued to spend.

Once the question was raised locally about how she could afford it, answers came thick and fast. It was said that she was well in with the smugglers and pirates that were about the Waterford coast in those days. It was also said that she was friendly with the highwaymen that prowled the roads. The rumour was that the secret rooms in the house were used for storing contraband and loot. And there were other stories too, of tunnels that led down from the House to the coves and bays below. Smuggled goods, unloaded from boats, were carried along these tunnels to safe locations.

Before long, Madam had turned the fine house at Ardo into a thieves' den, frequented only by criminals and outcasts. When pirate ships sheltered in the bays and inlets around Ardmore, their crews came ashore and made their way up to Ardo where they knew they'd be safe from the law.

The Madam held grand parties for all these rogues and robbers, well away from the eyes of local people. Many of those that attended were wanted by the authorities — but the Madam put up such a front that no-one dared to question her. For letting these rogues use the house, the Madam was believed to get a substantial amount of their booty and that was how she managed to keep up appearances.

Nobody can rightly say what was happening up in Ardo House, but there were certainly evil goings-on. There was even some talk of children disappearing from the houses round about. For her own part, the Madam never seemed to care much for children. She kept her two weak-minded younger children, Jeremiah and Thomasina, locked in their rooms.

As if its reputation as a den of thieves and robbers wasn't enough, Ardo now began to be talked of as a haunted house as well. Late at night, local people claimed, they heard desperate yells from the grounds and the house itself. Perhaps they were the cries of Richard Costen as he dangled over the ravine, being slowly throttled by the reins of his own horse? Or perhaps they were the screams of the servant murdered in the dining room by Sir Francis Prendergast? No-one dared say.

In addition, the weeping of a young child was heard. Nobody knew a story concerning a child, but long after all the Coghlans had died out and renovations were being carried out at Ardo, the tiny skeleton of a baby was found under the floorboards. Local legend said that it was a bastard child of the Madam's, born to one of the ruffians that came about the place, and that she'd murdered it and hidden its body.

Meanwhile, the parties and gatherings continued at Ardo. As well as carousing with villains, the Madam had started to give grand balls for the gentry. These parties were usually well attended, for people were curious to see the inside of the house. It was known that the Madam could throw a grand party — no expense spared. These always featured a song or two by the Madam, for she had a fine singing voice. But even at these great occasions, the ghosts of Ardo intruded.

One old story tells that when guests were dining at a large banquet, queer ghostly laughter rang out, alarming everybody there. Some of the guests and many of the servants also claimed they saw strange shadows in the corridors. Eventually the Madam had to pay the servants extra to work at Ardo after a certain time in the evening.

Once, the Madam was singing in one of the rooms during a grand party when she was answered from somewhere else in the house by an unearthly voice singing the same melody. Everybody that was there heard it. Then, as they listened, the sound changed to the screams of poor Richard Costen, which grew louder and louder until they were deafening. The room fairly cleared after that, and the incident marked the end of the great social parties at Ardo. Although the Madam still tried to hold them, fewer and fewer from the locality came. Ardo's reputation was worsening.

After many years, the Madam's money dried up. The ruffians and villains melted away — maybe the ghosts about the old place drove them out. With nothing coming in and her name no good anywhere, Madam Coghlan faced destitution. The estate fell into neglect and ruin. It became overgrown and the wonderful house that the Madam had built began to crumble and fall in on itself. This was too much for Madam Coghlan; her heart gave out and she died.

Behind her, she left Jeremiah and Thomasina. The eccentric Jeremiah was moody and antisocial. He'd fly into fierce tempers and wouldn't speak, even to the servants. He'd often lock himself in his room for long periods, eating nothing. He'd walk the grounds of Ardo at all hours, even in the middle of the night. In his pockets, he kept a couple of dead kittens, which he carried with him everywhere.

His sister Thomasina was a midget and suffered from a curved spine. She also kept to her room for long periods, where she played obsessively with her dolls — even into her eighties. She was fearful of anybody that came near her, especially Catholics. A deeply religious Protestant, she suspected her Catholic servants of slyly trying to convert her. She and her brother shared a notion that the food they ate was 'poisoned' with holy water, and Thomasina believed that she saw Catholic priests waiting in the shadows of the house to steal her soul ...

It was Jeremiah who died first — a sad and lonely death. Thomasina lived on at Ardo and became a recluse. Although she lived until she was almost ninety, none of the people of the locality ever visited her.

After Thomasina died, the air of sadness and weariness about Ardo deepened. Through the Madam's daughter who had married the Duc de Castries, it passed into the hands of a Marshal MacMahon, their grandson and one-time President of France. He took little interest in Ardo, never visiting it and allowing its deterioration to continue unchecked.

Meanwhile many local people still claimed to hear the Madam singing in the ruined rooms on clear winter nights. The ghost of Jeremiah Coghlan was rumoured to ride the roads on a white horse, carrying a crimson banner in honour of the grand marriage of his daughter. To see this phantom signalled the death of the viewer within the year. Other stories claimed that the evil spectre of Sir Francis Prendergast prowled the woods close by, carrying away all those that it met. And of course, the dying screams of Richard Costen could still be heard echoing down from *Crooke an Heire* ...

Eventually Marshal MacMahon sold Ardo to a family by the name of McKenna. Sir Joseph McKenna was a banker and a politician from Dublin. He renovated the mansion as a retreat from the hurly-burly of city life, and Ardo experienced one last blaze of glory. Once again, the old place rang to the sound of parties. The house twinkled with many lights; torches illuminated the avenue and great lamps were hung on the gates. As to whether the McKennas were troubled by ghosts, no-one knows — they never complained and, anyway, they spent most of their time in Dublin. What is known is that they did not prosper at Ardo, even though life there was more settled than before. There was always sickness coming in and out of the house and Sir Joseph, particularly, suffered from severe fits of depression. In the end, the family moved away and left Ardo to its ghosts.

Ardo was sold on several times, but nobody ever really lived there again and the old place fell into irreversible ruin. People claimed that old Sir Francis Prendergast stalked the fallen walls as if he still owned them, and that Madam Coghlan sang desperately to herself in abandoned rooms. My ancient informant told me that his own father-in-law had heard the long-dead Miss Thomasina screaming at the servants, late in the evenings when he was cutting grass around the ruin. He advised me to avoid going anywhere near the ruin — not late in the evening at any rate. I sounded a nominal agreement.

After the old man had told me the story of Ardo, I offered to walk with him to the nearest pub and buy him a drink for his trouble. He declined. He was simply pleased to have told me the story — few people took an interest in such places nowadays, he said, and he'd a feeling that Ardo was about to be pulled down. He shook his head. All that history, lost under a developer's shovel, and only himself and his wife to remember what went on there. But then again, he reasoned brightly, maybe it was a good thing — after all, the old house did not hold happy memories. Bidding the old couple goodbye, I left them standing in front of their door and set out along the road.

As I walked, I decided that I wanted a better view of the ruined splendour that once was Ardo, so a little further on, I climbed a gate and cut across the fields towards the ruined mansion. It was far bigger than I'd expected, due to the Madam's additions, but an air of gloom hung over the fallen stones and ivy-covered towers. Shadows ran between the diseased-looking trees. I found my way barred by hedges, thickets of brambles and tall, stinging nettles. Everywhere around me the bushes rustled in an undetected wind. It was all too easy to imagine the whispers and cries of the restless spirits. In my mind's eye, I could see phantoms. Old Sir Francis Prendergast, or perhaps Madam Coghlan, and all those with whom they trafficked, waited in the darkness under the branches ...

On the very edge of the weed-choked estate, I found a chipped and partly broken stone angel, entwined by a garment of creeper. Further along, there was a dilapidated mausoleum belonging to the departed McKennas, the last inhabitants of that sad house. The inscription on the crumbling edifice summed up the brooding melancholy of the abandoned dead:

'My life is like a broken stair,

Winding round a ruined tower,

And leading nowhere.'

I felt a pervasive sense of despair threatening to overwhelm me. Unable to proceed any further, I turned and walked quickly away. A crow flew over my head, its harsh cry echoing through the gloom of the fading light. The mournful call of unseen birds seemed a fitting end to the old man's tale. As I walked, the ruined, creepered towers of Ardoginna House gradually faded into the late evening haze.

A few months ago, a friend who knows the area well wrote to me about Ardo. He had passed the site of the house and had found the edges of the estate blocked off with developers' fences. The rumour was that all remaining traces of Ardo were to be pulled down to make way for new buildings. My friend railed against Waterford County Council, resenting its neglect for the long history of the house and the area. I found myself wondering what would now happen to the remains of that ill-fated old house. Would they eventually be swept away along with their ghosts? Maybe they would finally form the foundations of happy, unhaunted homes for new inhabitants. Then again, maybe they wouldn't ...

The Touch of the Dead

'Oh ye Dead! oh ye Dead! whom we know by the light you give,
From your cold gleaming eyes, though you move like men who live.'

Thomas Moore, Irish Melodies, Vol. 8

We normally view ghosts as ethereal, shadowy images, either waft-
ing along corridors, wailing and bemoaning their fate, or infesting old
ruins, causing terror to all those who encounter them. However,
the idea of an insubstantial spirit is a fairly recent one, owing more to
Victorian ghost lore than to ancient traditions. In earlier times, particularly amongst the early Celtic peoples, ghosts were much more
substantial.

Ghosts were, after all, the revenants of friends, relatives and
neighbours, and they often continued to do all the things that
they'd done in life. For example, a dead cobbler might return
from the grave in order to mend shoes, and he would need to be
in a more corporeal form than the Victorian spectre of popular
myth in order to do this. It was also believed that the returning
dead could eat, so food was often left out for them on special
occasions, such as the feast day known as *Fáilte na Marbh* (the

Welcoming of the Dead, or Hallowe'en). It was even believed that those who returned from the grave could claim conjugal rights ...

The Celtic dead were therefore very substantial entities. They could touch and be touched, although the touch of their ice-cold fingers would leave a mark similar to a burn. Many years ago, an old lady showed me what appeared to be a burn mark on the wall of her house – a small, dark, circular stain – which she told me was the handprint of one of the returning dead that had touched the stonework in some former time. Occasionally, the lady explained, the mark and the area around it gave off a feeling of coldness. This was, she claimed, a legacy of the dead.

The hand of a ghost, it is said, always has an effect upon what it touches – whether that be an item or a person. Even the very passing of the dead can cause milk to turn sour, bread to turn mouldy or food to turn rotten. If a ghost or a walking corpse were to touch a living person, that person would be 'marked for life'. This ghastly imprint features in a number of ghost stories in the North, one of the most famous of which is the story of Lady Nicola Beresford of Gill Hall, County Down.

Although Gill Hall is no longer standing, in its heyday it was a grand and imposing mansion. A photograph of it – possibly the last before it was mysteriously burned down – appears in the Dromore Leader for 6 June 1966. It shows a majestic edifice in its own sumptuous grounds. But even in this photograph, obviously taken on a glorious summer's day, an air of menace hangs over the place, adding to its one-time reputation as 'the most haunted house in Ireland'.

Gill Hall was originally built around 1670 by John Magill. He was a member of the prosperous Hawkins-Magill family who had been granted lands by the Crown in the excellent farming country around Dromore, County Down. The house was enlarged in 1731, by which time its sinister reputation was firmly in place.

The haunting of Gill Hall involves two members of the seventeenth-century Irish aristocracy: Lady Nicola Sophie Hamilton and John Power, more commonly known as Lord Tyrone. Lady Nicola came from an old, established Planter family. She was a lively and intelligent girl in her youth, who far outstripped many of her contemporaries in the fields of philosophy and religion — unusual interests for a girl in the 1600s. The second Earl of Tyrone was a rather shy, intellectual young man, who sought the company of more learned people than himself.

Since Lord Tyrone and Lady Nicola went to the same school, it was only natural that they should strike up a friendship, which, through all the years that they were together, remained platonic. They discussed many topics, from science to philosophy and religion. Both of them had a keen interest in astrology and in the possibility of reincarnation. Lady Nicola especially took these subjects to heart and became almost obsessed with the question of whether or not there was life after death.

'There must be some way that we can find out if there is something beyond the grave,' said Lord Tyrone one evening as they discussed certain religious matters. 'Let's make a pact. Whichever one of us dies first will come back and tell the other if there is, indeed, an Afterlife.'

'An excellent idea!' exclaimed Lady Nicola. 'Let's swear it now. Whoever dies first will come back and speak to the other.' And so the macabre agreement was made.

Time passed and the bargain was all but forgotten. Gradually Lady Nicola and Lord Tyrone drifted apart and began to pursue their own lives. Lady Nicola married Tristram Beresford, the son of an influential Plantation family who were related to the Bishops of Dromore. Lord Tyrone more or less withdrew from public life and became a virtual recluse.

On a mid-October morning in 1693, while Lady Nicola and her husband were staying as guests at Gill Hall, the lady came down to breakfast looking so drawn and pale, she seemed ill. About her right wrist, she wore a band of black velvet. Concerned that she had somehow injured herself, her host asked about it. Lady Nicola became agitated, refused to answer any questions and told her astonished sister and husband that, if they cared for her, they should never ask about it again.

From that day until the day that she died, Lady Nicola was never without a black band around her right wrist. Her request was observed and, throughout her life, those in her company were warned never to mention her hand. Nor did she ever again regain her youthful spirit and vivacity. Instead, she turned into a grim, prematurely aged matron, who seemed to be continually looking over her shoulder.

Before certain life events, such as the birth of her son and the death of Sir Tristram, it was noted that Lady Nicola's agitation would return. As she approached her forty-seventh birthday, she became so agitated, she was almost hysterical but, when the birthday passed, she sank into deep depression.

'I shall never see another birthday,' was her blunt reply, when asked what was wrong.

Knowing that she was in good health, her friends only laughed at her. They told her she was still a young woman and to put such morbid thoughts from her mind. However, several months later, Lady Nicola fulfilled her own prediction, when she sickened and, soon after, died. Some of her friends declared that she'd simply willed herself to death.

Lady Nicola's own end was not the first prophecy that she'd uttered, nor the first death that she'd foretold. Many years before — the day after that fateful October breakfast when she'd come down with her black-bandaged wrist — Lady Nicola had asked one of the servants if there'd been any letter addressed to her delivered to Gill Hall.

'No, ma'am,' answered the girl. 'No post yet today.'

'Then it will most probably come tomorrow,' Lady Nicola muttered, as if to herself.

'Why do you want to know, Nicola?' her brother-in-law enquired. Lady Nicola had paused for a moment, as if considering what to tell him.

'I'm awaiting news of the death of Lord Tyrone,' she finally replied.

Her host gazed at her blankly.

'But Lord Tyrone isn't dead!' he protested. 'I chanced to run across him in Dublin just over a month ago and he was hale and hearty.'

Lady Nicola remained unmoved.

'His death was very sudden,' she said. 'It happened only yesterday, on the fourteenth of October, sometime after four a.m.' Her host's wonder deepened. News in Ireland travelled slowly, and he was certain that Lady Nicola hadn't heard from Lord Tyrone in some time. How could she have heard anything about him so quickly? And how did she know the exact date and time of his death? Lady Nicola, however, passed no further comment on the matter.

Two days later, a letter arrived at Gill Hall, which communicated the news that Lord Tyrone was dead and that he'd died in Dublin, early on the previous Tuesday — the fourteenth of October 1693, at four a.m.

It was only on her deathbed that Lady Nicola revealed the astonishing truth to her relatives. First of all, she told them about the pact that had been made between herself and Tyrone all those years before. And then she moved on to a terrifying story.

On the morning of the fourteenth of October 1693, Sir Tristram had risen and went to the study in Gill Hall to complete some paperwork, leaving Lady Nicola alone in the bedroom. It was about seven or eight a.m. and the gloomy morning light was just starting to steal in. As she lay in bed, Lady Nicola suddenly felt very cold and the drapes around the bedposts stirred as if a wind had moved them. Surprised, and a little frightened, she peered out into the dim room.

Between the window and her bed, a shadowy figure was standing. Though she couldn't see who it was, she knew it to be a man — a man who was not her husband. With a trembling hand, she reached for the candle by her bed, to hold it up for a better look.

'Who ... who is it?' she stammered in a quavering voice. 'Who's there?'

The figure made a motion with its hand to stay where she was and not to be afraid.

'Surely you know an old friend?' he said in low, sad tones. 'One who won't do you any harm!'

Lady Nicola stared in amazement for she knew the voice — it was that of her childhood companion, Lord Tyrone. He stepped forward into the pale daylight that was easing itself into the room and she recognised him straight away. He was just as she remembered him the last time that she'd seen him, but he looked rather gaunt and pale. Assuming that Lord Tyrone had arrived unexpectedly at Gill Hall the night before, Lady Nicola relaxed a little.

'When did you arrive?' she asked. 'And what brings you to Gill Hall?' Lord Tyrone sighed — a long, dreary sound.

'Surely you haven't forgotten the pact that we made all that time ago when we were at school together?' his spirit answered. 'That whoever died first would come back to assure the other of the ... the Afterlife? That's why I've come back to you.'

When Lady Nicola heard this, she realised she was talking to the dead and the hairs on the nape of her neck prickled.

'And you've come to tell me that there is an Afterlife?' she managed to blurt out. 'Your very presence here confirms it, for I believe you to be a — a ghost!' She could barely bring herself to speak the word. The shape nodded sadly.

'There is indeed an Afterlife,' he replied ponderously, 'But it is not what we expect it to be. I am expressly forbidden to tell you anything more, save of its existence.'

'But how do I know that you're a real ghost?' asked Lady Nicola.

'To prove to you that I am who I say I am, I am permitted to demonstrate my power of prophecy. I can tell you some of the things that will befall you in life.'

The phantom then proceeded to prophesy that Lady Nicola would bear Sir Tristram a son; that shortly afterwards her husband would die; that she would marry again; and that she herself would die at the age of forty-seven.

But Lady Nicola still wasn't sure. 'Give me proof that you are from beyond the grave! What was the exact hour of your death?'

The ghost considered. 'I'm permitted to tell you that I died in Dublin at four o'clock this morning,' he said at length. 'I can give you more proof, if you desire. Give me your pocket book and a pen.'

Crossing to her bureau, the ghost took up the pocket book and wrote in it in a broad, flowing script that Lady Nicola immediately recognised as Lord Tyrone's handwriting.

'There!' said the ghost handing the book and pen back. 'That'll confirm to you that I've been here.'

Lady Nicola was still very dubious about her visitor. He seemed far too solid to be a ghost! 'You seem real enough to me – a man of flesh and blood – like any living creature. How do I know I'm not dreaming, or that this isn't some elaborate trick that you've hatched with my sister?'

'There's only one more proof that I can offer – but I'm loathe to give it!' the ghost replied in agitation.

Lady Nicola took the book and looked at the name that had been written there. It looked like Tyrone's handwriting, and yet ...

'Give me this final proof that you mentioned,' she demanded.

The ghost looked mournful. 'If I give it, it's a proof that you must carry to the grave.'

Lady Nicola swallowed. 'Then do it!' she answered. 'Or I'll doubt this moment forever!'

The ghost looked very solemn. 'Well, then! Stretch out your right hand towards me!'

Nervously, Lady Nicola did as she was told and she noticed that her hand trembled. Looking into the face of the ghost in front of her, she saw that his eyes burned with an inner fire and that he looked gaunt to the point of being skeletal. Reaching forward, he gripped her wrist in his own hand.

His deathly touch was horribly cold — so cold that it seemed to burn her skin with a terrible fire. Lady Nicola screamed in pain and the ghost let go quickly. Looking down, she saw that the sinews on her right wrist had withered and shrivelled, and that the skin around the area was now discoloured. She could clearly see the black marks where her ghastly visitor had touched her.

'That is a mark between us,' said the phantom sadly. 'And it must remain between us for the rest of your life. No-one can ever see it, not even your husband. It is your certainty of the Afterlife and yours alone. All is as agreed!'

'Can't I show it even to my sister?' queried Lady Nicola.

But the spectre shook his head. 'It must remain a personal bond between the two of us and no-one else,' he said. 'And you will cover it forthwith and let none see it. You must never mention it until you are ready to cross over. Will you give me your word?'

Lady Nicola nodded dumbly.

'Good,' said the ghost. 'Then I've fulfilled our pact and must depart. If you ever doubt what has happened this day, look upon the mark on your wrist, for it is the touch of the dead. My name in your book will fade with time, but the mark will remain forever. I bid you farewell, old friend!'

There was a sound like a rushing wind and, in an instant, the figure had gone. Lady Nicola was alone in the bedroom once more. But when she looked at her wrist, she saw that the marks of Lord Tyrone's ghostly fingers were still there, turning even blacker as the seconds passed. Going over to her workbasket, she took out a large piece of black velvet from which she tore a strip. Wrapping it round her wrist, she made a makeshift band and from that day onwards, it was never removed, save for bathing which she did alone.

And so she kept her secret until she was on her deathbed, when she felt able to reveal the tale of the ghost in her bedroom. Even then, though, she did not remove the band around her wrist. It was only when she was in her coffin that her son took the strip of velvet away and saw that the marks of Lord Tyrone's fingers were still clearly visible.

This is the tale, which passed not only down through the Beresford family, but also into local folklore. Such was its impact on the local imagination that, over the years, Gill Hall acquired the darkest of reputations. The ghost of Lord Tyrone was said to be seen about the place, either at one of the windows looking languidly down, or in the grounds of the house. The phantom was sometimes joined, in the popular mind, by the spectre of Lady Nicola Beresford herself, a ghost that darted quickly along the shadowy corridors of Gill Hall or came and went from room to room, loudly banging doors in its wake.

There are other tales, too, concerning a ghostly hand wrapped in a black velvet band that drifts through the hallway and upper rooms of the Hall on certain nights of the year — particularly around the middle of October. This disembodied hand was also sometimes accompanied by a drifting shadow which could be seen either early in the morning or last thing at night. An aunt of my own once told me that she'd spoken to a workman who'd been in the house late in the evening and had actually seen the hand clutching at the banister on the great staircase. The vision, he went on to say, was accompanied by a kind of whispering sound, which seemed to fill the hallway where he was working. The man was so frightened that he fled from the place, according to my aunt, without even retrieving his tools.

During the eighteenth and nineteenth centuries, Gill Hall continued to be inhabited despite its increasingly dubious associations. By the mid-twentieth century, however, it was more or less abandoned, and fully came into its own as a 'haunted house'. It is not recorded whether the Americans that were quartered there for part of the Second World War saw or heard anything. However, my aunt, who occasionally visited Gill Hall after the Americans had gone, claimed to have had 'queer experiences' herself in the gloomy and desolate place it had become. One time, she sensed someone looking down on her from one of the uncurtained upstairs windows as she walked around the now overgrown grounds. For many years afterwards, she talked of seeing a figure there, even though she knew the old house to be completely empty. On a number of other occasions, she noticed a previously closed door standing wide open, as though inviting her in. She never took up the invitation. Few people, she assured me, would go anywhere near the old mansion except during daylight hours.

I visited Gill Hall myself, one Sunday afternoon in the early 1960s. My school friends and I were all learning to drive — a couple of us had actually passed our driving test — and, with youthful bravado, we decided to drive out to the ancient house to look for the famous ghosts that were supposed to haunt it. Since the house was infamous, the visit became a kind of impetuous 'dare' between us all. We went one overcast summer's evening.

Gill Hall had an almost palpable air of menace. Parking our cars on the roadway that ran along the edge of the estate, we entered through a break in the fence and made our way across the extensive grounds. After exploring the surrounding area, we set about finding a way into the brooding house. Wandering around the outside several times, we passed the door that my aunt had talked about. It was closed. Then, round the back, one of us found a window on the second floor that was partly open and could be levered up. There was a bit of a scramble up the wall as the most agile of our group climbed up to the opening, pushed it up and helped the rest of us in. I was one of the last to climb up. Clambering awkwardly through the aperture, I joined my friends in the dim, cobwebby interior.

We had come through into a small room at the back of the house. The room was completely empty except for a couple of packing cases marked 'U.S. Army Stores'. A few other unmarked, broken crates lay against a wall on the other side of the room. Almost opposite us was a great door with peeling paint, which led to another part of the house. It, too, was tightly closed. The walls all around us had been painted a sterile and uniform grey that only added to the sense of gloom and oppression. Although the evening was rather clammy, we all felt cold. Between the window and the door, the uncarpeted floorboards looked weak and rotten. We wondered whether we should venture across them.

Eventually myself and one of the others decided to chance the floor and see if we could open the door at the other side. It proved stiff but at last the handle turned and we stepped out into what looked like a back corridor. To our right, was another plain grey wall against which was propped another packing case and a large empty cardboard box, similarly marked to those in the other room. To our left, the corridor stretched away to another door. Two dirty windows further along allowed a dirty twilight to fall on the floor, showing that part of it had fallen away and was extremely unsafe.

Along the left-side wall, there were several other doors, two with broken panelling. Someone had scrawled graffiti across one of them in what looked like chalk or white crayon. The door directly opposite opened onto a broken part of the floor, so we couldn't investigate. I tried one of the other, nearer doors but it was firmly locked. I thought about trying another, but then I felt the floorboards give beneath my feet and turned back.

The sense of oppression in the corridor was almost tangible. Maybe it was the dirt of the windows or the failing light outside that added to this impression, but I felt as though the shadows further along moved and shifted of their own volition. Throughout my time in the house, I had the oddest feeling that there was someone else nearby, watching us. But I knew it was just the atmosphere of the old house — nothing more than a sensation brought on by an adolescent imagination and a sinister reputation. Yet, years later, even as I'm writing this, I can't help but suppress a shudder at the memory.

There was a faint noise elsewhere in the building, which startled both my friend and me. It sounded like a door closing or something falling. It frightened us both, so we scuttled back to the room to find that most of our friends had already departed. The awful atmosphere of the house had apparently got to them as well. I don't think that any of us took the time to climb back down from the open window — we all jumped. Then we ran as fast as we could across the grounds and back to our cars.

Later, I tried to tell myself that our fear was because we'd be caught trespassing — we were all there illegally and the grounds were supposedly private — but, in reality, I think that we had all been deeply disturbed by the atmosphere of Gill Hall.

Although none of us admitted it — in fact, later we all made a great joke of the whole experience — the house had frightened each one of us.

We've all gone our separate ways now, and are no longer in touch but, through the facility of memory, the eerie visit to Gill Hall unites us still. Although I myself have visited many 'haunted houses' over the years, I've never experienced the same sensation of creeping horror as I did on that overcast summer's evening.

Around the beginning of the 1970s, Gill Hall was burned down. Today, there is no trace of the once-great house. How the fire actually started remains a mystery — a popular explanation is that the house was being used as a shelter by tramps who accidentally began the blaze — but it's unlikely that anybody will ever know the true facts.

A portrait of Lady Nicola Beresford hung for many years in the privately owned Tyrone House, opposite Dublin's Pro-Cathedral in Marlborough Street (now the Department of Education). I'm told that it showed the black band round her wrist where Tyrone's ghost shrivelled her sinews — the touch of the dead that she carried with her to the grave. And in a sense, I felt that the dead also touched myself and my friends that summer's evening several centuries later. To some extent, the dead retain the power to touch us all, whether or not we recognise it. Perhaps even in this busy modern world, the shades of our ancestors are closer than we suspect.

The Haunted Castle of Leap

'All houses are haunted where men have lived and died.'

So runs an old country saying – but some buildings are more haunted than others. These are places that have seen such tragedy, despair or violence that the living may pick up the vibrations of persons or scenes long gone.

In rural Ireland, it is widely believed that an already haunted building may attract other phantoms and other supernatural beings. A number of objects can draw such unwelcome beings to a house – the unwashed clothes of a 'scandalous' woman, religious artefacts that have been stolen or misappropriated, blood spilled in anger, or even mouldy food or dirty crockery. Of this list, it is the spilling of blood that is the most potently evil. One example of how violence can forever mar the spirit of a building is that of Carrigaphouka Castle, two miles west of Macroom, County Cork.

Carrigaphouka Castle (meaning 'rock of the *puca*', or evil spirit) is a four-storey, fifteenth-century edifice, now in ruins. It was once the stronghold of a branch of the MacCarthy clan. In 1601, the castle was the fortress of Cormac Tadhg MacCarthy, who, having accepted a knighthood from the English, became Sheriff of Cork. His remit was to aid in the hunting down and apprehension of a number of Irish 'rebels' who had allegedly taken part in the uprising of Red Hugh O'Neill. Together with Sir Walter Raleigh and Sir Warham St. Leger, Cormac surprised and captured the one such rebel, James Fitzgerald. He supervised his traitor's death, which featured his being dismembered while still alive. Some variations of the story say that Cormac actually ate Fitzgerald's flesh and drank his blood to demonstrate his loyalty to the English. In any case, this terrible and bloodthirsty act was to cause Cormac's ghost to haunt the castle forever, attacking its inhabitants and drinking their blood.

Carrigaphouka Castle was held by Cormac's descendants until 1690 when it was confiscated during the Williamite Wars in Ireland. It subsequently slid into abandonment and decay. It maintained its sinister reputation and is, even today, deemed to be so badly haunted that few locals will approach it after dark. As recently as 1993, an article in the October edition of *Ireland's Eye* magazine noted that it was '… a place of ghosts and fairies. The country folk around would report that strange cries and noises came from the depths of the castle. People returning from fairs and markets would hasten their steps when passing the place before the strange lights at midnight would appear'.

In Cormac Tadhg's defence, the MacCarthys have always claimed that an earlier, malignant spirit, a *puca*, emerged from the rock on which the castle was built and possessed him, making him commit these hideous acts. They say that this same ancient spirit haunts the rock still, always on the lookout for fresh victims to possess and manipulate.

Another extremely haunted place in Ireland, and indeed recently judged as one of the most haunted places in Western Europe, lies between the towns of Birr in County Offaly and Roscrea in County Tipperary. Some say Leap Castle stands on a spot where a number of ancient 'ley-lines' (lines of primal force) intersect. It has acquired the most sinister of reputations across its long history – a history that is bathed in blood …

To the casual passer-by, Leap Castle, deep in a small valley and surrounded by the scattered remnants of prehistoric forts, is no different from any other of the ancient castles that dot the Irish midlands. It once guarded a strategic pass through the Slieve Bloom mountains, connecting the coast with the plains of Leix and Offaly. Control of such places was vital in Ireland during the fifteenth and sixteenth centuries when the times were unsettled and trade was precarious. This mountain route was being fought over by various factions seeking to use it for military purposes. The area around the Slieve Bloom mountains was often a bloody battlefield, just the place for ghosts and dark creatures. To understand why Leap Castle should be so badly haunted, it is necessary to know a little of its turbulent and blood-soaked history.

The first 'overlord' of the area was the Norman knight Theobald Fitzwalter, but other Irish clans thrived, many of whom took Norman names, such as O'Carrig, Fanning, Lawless, Purcell and O'Bannion. But it was another, more ferocious sept which left its mark on the area. They were the O'Carrolls — 'the dark princes of Ely', a name by which that area of Offaly was originally known.

The O'Carrolls were a northern clan — possibly from the border area around Tyrone, Monaghan and the Slieve Beigh mountains — who had been pushed south by an expansion of the O'Neills in Ulster. Tracing their lineage from Cearbell, a ninth-century Irish king, they were described as a 'lordly sept'. As settlers, they seem to have been savage, driving all the indigenous clans away to establish themselves in the area. It was around this time that Leap Castle, arguably the most strategically important fortress in the Irish midlands, was built. It is highly probable that Leap was built on the site of an earlier fortification, dating from the Iron Age.

The name 'Leap' is puzzling, but one explanation for it may be found in a gory piece of local folklore. The full name of the site is *Léim Uí Bhannain*, or the Leap of O'Bannion. Tradition states that when the O'Carrolls seized the lands, the O'Bannions were the indigenous clan. They refused to pay tribute to their new overlords and so the O'Carrolls made them an offer. There was a place on their newly acquired lands, they said, where two great rocks rose out of the ground near an ancient earthen fort. If the O'Bannions could produce a champion who could leap between these rocks, they would be excused their tribute forever. If their champion fell, then the O'Bannions must accept the O'Carrolls as their masters.

The feat was agreed and an O'Bannion champion came forward, only to miss the jump and be dashed to pieces on the rocks below. The O'Carrolls then turned on the O'Bannions, slaughtering many of their best men. They seized the O'Bannion lands and built Leap Castle on the site where the champion had perished. In a macabre and grisly addition to the tale, it's said that they used some of his blood in order to mix the mortar for the building's foundation stones. This gave rise to the motto that hangs over the place: 'Raised in blood, blood be its portion'. This awful legend is just one of the explanations for the odd name of the fortress. Other stories maintain the notion of a 'leap' between two rocks, but lay the blame squarely with the O'Bannions themselves, suggesting that such a jump was a method by which a new chieftain was chosen and that many perished on the site because of their own ambition.

Whether or not the place was cursed, it seemed it was certainly unlucky for many of the early O'Carroll chieftains. More than a few of them died within its grim walls from something which the chroniclers describe as 'the creeping plague', a strange wasting disease that seems to have taken its victims to a slow and lingering death. In 1489, John O'Carroll died 'most horribly' at Leap from an ailment referred to in records as the 'bloody flux and a pox'. Elderly locals further point to the fact that, in order to construct the castle, the O'Carrolls destroyed several prehistoric sites, and cut into a large and ancient earthworks. No good, the old people argue, could surely have come of disturbing these possibly sacred places and of disturbing the ancestral spirits.

Leap had always been important but, in the sixteenth century, it also acquired a bloody and sinister reputation. As the English sought to increase their influence beyond the Pale of Dublin and develop farming lands in North Tipperary, the midlands became an important strategic area. Two factions had emerged in the region — the Fitzgerald Earls of Desmond and Kildare, who considered themselves ancient Gaelic aristocracy; and the Butler Dukes of Ormond and North Tipperary who were, in the main, pro-English. Around these two great houses, the Irish chieftains clustered, taking sides between them, often splitting clans down the middle and turning brother against brother. The centre of Ireland became a blood-soaked buffer zone, with the O'Carrolls acting as power brokers between the warring factions of Offaly. Leap Castle, described by the Earl of Desmond as 'the best-defended castle in Ireland', assumed an even greater significance.

In 1541, following a period of intense in-fighting, Leap Castle passed into the hands of Tadhg Coach O'Carroll, known as One-Eyed Tadhg.

One-Eyed Tadhg was not the eldest of his immediate family and not the most obvious heir to Ely. He was already at war with a cousin, Calvagh O'Carroll, over territorial matters, and he had at least two elder brothers who should have taken precedence over him. However, John O'Carroll was weak-minded and therefore unfit to lead the O'Carrolls, while Thaddeus McFir O'Carroll was considered incapable of the necessary ruthless leadership because he was a priest. But Thaddeus MacFir was backed by the powerful Earls of Desmond and, despite his Holy Orders, he was a skilled and clever politician. His dabbling often brought him into conflict with his younger brother, Tadhg.

There is no doubt that Tadhg was a vicious mass-murderer. As the prospective leader of his clan, he sought to extend the borders of the Kingdom of Ely through a programme of slaughter and burning. He created treaties with James the Lame, the Duke of Ormond, in order to gain Butler support for his murderous activities. Meanwhile, however, his brother Thaddeus had been negotiating with the opposing Fitzgerald faction and was undermining Tadhg at every turn. Tadhg decided that some action was needed, so he invited his brother to use the chapel at Leap Castle as his own personal religious sanctuary.

The chapel at Leap still lies at the very top of a central tower, and is accessed by a winding stone staircase. It is small as chapels go, but would have provided an excellent sanctuary for prayer and contemplation. Tadhg, however, had other ideas. As his brother knelt in prayer at the altar rail, Tadhg crept into the chapel and slit his throat. This act of murder was also an act of blasphemy, and ensured the damnation of One-Eyed Tadhg O'Carroll.

With his brother out of the way, Tadhg's excesses became even more horrendous. He embarked on a programme of unparalleled killing and pillage. One of the most notorious stories about him concerns the action he took against the O'Mahons (also called the McMahons), who had settled in the area and who had been supporters of Tadhg's brother Thaddeus.

During a lull in hostilities between Tadhg and the O'Mahons, Tadhg made overtures of peace, and invited about forty O'Mahon clan members to a grand banquet at Leap Castle. Of course, he had no intention of allowing them to leave alive. The food and the wine he gave them were drugged and, as the O'Mahons succumbed to the effects, Tadhg had them carried one by one to the chapel.

There, in the chapel wall, Tadhg had built a long shaft known as an oubliette, which dropped steeply all the way down to the basement of the castle. Prisoners were thrown into the oubliette, bricked up, and forgotten. In the case of the McMahons, Tadhg had also lined the sides of the oubliette with metal spikes. Those McMahons who were conscious demanded to be thrown down head first, hoping to break their necks on the ground rather than die slowly on the spikes. The oubliette remained sealed until the mid-1920s; when it was finally excavated, four cartloads of human remains — all that was left of the O'Mahon clan — were taken away.

After Tadhg had seized the O'Mahon lands and increased his territory, now known as 'Ely O'Carroll', the English in Dublin became seriously alarmed. They sent an army under the command of Edmund Fahy. Unfortunately Fahy was let down by his allies and had to face the full fury of Tadhg with a skeleton army. The inevitable rout included a comprehensive defeat for Fahy at Carrigahorrig on the Shannon. Tadhg burned several towns that were sheltering troops, including Nenagh, and took scores of prisoners. Back at Leap Castle, Tadhg put his prisoners in a network of underground dungeons stretching for miles, sealing the doors to their cells and leaving them to starve in lightless tombs. The cells are still there, unopened since that day, although the rock passages that access them are now impassable. Only the rats come and go at will.

In 1552, Tadhg made peace with the English and accepted a knighthood, but the internal disputes amongst the O'Carrolls continued to rage. In securing an English title for himself, Tadhg had incurred the enmity of his surviving brothers. Urged on by these brothers, Tadhg's old enemy, Calvagh O'Carroll, attacked and murdered Tadhg in 1553, bringing to an end his bloodthirsty overlordship. In 1688, the O'Carroll clan finally left the area in return for a grant of sixty thousand acres in Maryland in the United States of America. Their ancestral lands became part of the English Plantation.

Once again, a bizarre and colourful character became master of Leap Castle. Jonathan Darby, known as 'the Wild Captain', was a staunch Royalist of eccentric and immoral habits. He strengthened his claim on the area around the Slieve Bloom mountains by marrying an O'Carroll princess, and is said to have abused wife, servants and tenants alike. Darby became infamous for the wild, orgiastic parties he held at Leap Castle.

One of the stories about Darby concerned his fortune of gold and precious stones, which he hid in a secret chamber in the castle. With the help of two loyal servants, vast quantities of wealth had been transported and stored in this hidden room. When this was done, he murdered both the servants and bricked up their bodies somewhere within the castle. Shortly afterwards, however, Darby was arrested and imprisoned in Dublin on an alleged charge of treason. When released, many years later, he was on the edge of madness and had completely forgotten where he had hidden his fortune. It has never been discovered to this day. What was eventually discovered, however, were two upright skeletons bricked behind a wall.

The Darbys added extensions to the basic O'Carroll tower-house. They built wings containing more rooms and another chapel (by now the original chapel, known as 'the Bloody Chapel', had been shut up). Even then, the place had not shaken off it atmosphere. Builders complained that they could hear the anguished screams of Edmund Fahy's soldiers coming from below ground level. At night, children could be heard crying somewhere away in the depths of the castle. In one bedroom, guests were sometimes woken by the terrifying spectre of a tall, female figure, dressed in what appeared to be a red gown, her right hand raised threateningly and a hellish fire burning around her head. This was believed to be the ghost of an O'Carroll princess — perhaps the one that Jonathan Darby had married, or perhaps an earlier soul who had died in the castle.

Generations of Darbys added to the castle, building on Gothic wings and additional rooms. During this later period, a phantom monk was supposed to roam the corridors. A little old man of antique garb — green cut-away coat, knee breeches and buckled shoes — was sometimes also seen, occasionally accompanied by an elderly lady in a similarly old-fashioned costume. Footsteps were heard in various parts of the place, and a mysterious cloaked figure often prowled the grounds close to the walls.

And, of course, there was the Bloody Chapel itself, into which few of the workmen would venture. Although it was never used, an eerie light could be seen in its window from away across the valley. Legend stated that behind its doors, the cursed ghost of Tadhg O'Carroll still lurked, ready to sneak up behind those who approached the altar, slash their throats and drink their blood. It also still contained the sealed oubliette, in which lay the bodies of the dead O'Mahons, whose unquiet phantoms haunted the upper sections of the stone tower-house.

The castle had such a growing and sinister reputation that it seems even the later Darbys themselves shunned the place, spending long periods in their properties in England. In effect, they became absentee landlords, visiting Leap only infrequently. During a prolonged absence, during the Civil War in the early 1920s, Leap Castle was attacked and burned by the IRA. Local tradition says that the castle's peacocks, which had long strutted through the grounds, were captured and crucified. Many of the newer parts of the castle, extensions that the Darbys had built, went up in flames. The central tower-house however, despite some damage, remained largely intact and forms the centrepiece of the castle today.

The ghosts haven't gone away. The ghostly O'Carroll princess is still said to appear from time to time in what is now called the State Bedroom and, even today, few people will enter the Bloody Chapel for fear of meeting the murdering phantom of Tadhg O'Carroll. A resident of the gate-lodge told me that, on clear moonlit nights, she often saw two young girls, playing on the open ground in front of the deserted castle. But the most frightening of all the beings that have haunted the site over the years is not a ghost at all, but an 'elemental'.

An elemental is a creature that has never lived, but is composed of primeval malignant forces. It is charactised by an exceptionally foul smell, like the stench of rotting carrion. The Thing, as it has come to be known, is usually invisible. At Leap, it is said to lurk around a turn of the spiral staircase leading to the Bloody Chapel, ready to throw unwary visitors down the stone steps. Only a few people have ever actually seen the Thing, one of whom was a Miss Darby who owned the castle at the time.

Miss Darby was walking along a short passageway that ran from the staircase to one of the bedrooms. She smelled a horrible stench and then, in the gloom, glimpsed a hideous creature. She described it as being about four feet high, roughly human in shape and seemingly composed of iron-grey cotton wool. Two dark, glittering eyes, likes holes in its face, glared at her malevolently. On this occasion Miss Darby was fortunate: she managed to repel the Thing's attack on her, and it disappeared, leaving a sickening smell in its wake.

Another description, given by a guest at Leap, tells of a man-size figure with what looked like the skull of a sheep as its head and a shaggy, black-furred body with two great paw-like hands. There was no attack on this occasion, but again the guest commented on the creature's terrible reek.

The reputation of Leap Castle has become so widespread that mediums and spiritualists from all around the world have beaten a path to its doors. Psychics from as far away as Mexico and Japan have visited the place. Through them, we have a little information about some of the phantoms that inhabit the ruin. It has been suggested, for instance, that the two ghostly girls might be the spectres of two children who lived at the castle in the early 1800s, one of whom was killed in a fall from the tower. The other child had a withered leg and was lame. The girls are not malign spirits — although there are others who prowl the corridor and grounds that are. So bad is the atmosphere in places that some mediums have refused to enter the castle, sensing blood everywhere, and one or two have become quite hysterical.

The Darbys are no longer the owners of Leap. The castle was given to an old family retainer — an eccentric and reclusive old lady with a limp, whose ghost has also been seen within its precincts. It then passed through the hands of several owners, none of whom stayed long and none of whom appear to have prospered. One owner, Peter Gerrard, who owned Leap between 1973 and 1975, claimed that the land around the place was 'bad'. He himself lost money on its sale and, shortly afterwards, died tragically.

Today, the musician Sean Ryan and his family live at Leap Castle. Although much of the castle lies in ruins, Sean is in the process of restoring much of the damage done to the central tower-house during the Irish Civil War. He is aware of the ghosts that haunt his home but says that they do him no harm. In fact, his daughters sometimes play with the two ghostly girls, whom they can see very clearly — though adults can see them only dimly. Despite the alleged curse that is said to hang over the fortress from the days of the O'Bannions, Sean and his family are happy there. Nevertheless, interest in the sinister reputation of the place does not diminish — recently the Psychic Society accorded Leap the dubious honour of being 'the most haunted place in Western Europe'.

In June 2002, I visited Leap to take part in a programme for the RTÉ 'Townlands' series. With a TV crew, we sat by the fire in the castle's great hall whilst Sean regaled us with stories of the place's macabre history. One of his stories concerned the oubliette in the Bloody Chapel. Apparently, when the oubliette was being cleared out in the 1920s, a gentleman's pocket watch was found on one of the skeletons. Since such an item could not have existed in the sixteenth century when it was thought the shaft had been sealed, the implication was that there'd been at least one more murder committed at Leap during the ownership of the Darbys, and the body was dumped inside the oubliette.

Later, we were joined by the Northern ghost hunter, Barry Fitzgerald, who declared that Leap Castle was the 'most haunted place' he'd ever visited. Barry reported that, while setting up equipment in a darkened anteroom off the Bloody Chapel, he had become aware of something big, dark and bulky watching him fixedly from further back in the room. The shape quickly moved away as he himself moved towards it. In addition, his sound crew had heard odd voices talking close by, even though they were by themselves in the chapel. Finally, they reported a noise as though chains were being dragged across the floor of the room, even though there was nothing to be seen.

For myself, while standing in front of the oubliette to deliver a piece directly to camera, I suddenly felt a touch like an incredibly cold hand on the base of my spine. In a moment the sensation had vanished, but there was no doubt that I had experienced it. Of course, it might have been a sudden chilling gust of air through the glassless windows, but there was no wind that day. As I went over to look out of the high window, I felt the momentary urge to throw myself from the height into the ruins below ... I wondered if the child who had 'fallen' from the upper window of the tower had had the same impulse. All in all, I was glad to leave Leap Castle behind me, especially when I heard that the night after we'd left, the eerie light occasionally seen in the Bloody Chapel was said to be burning as brightly as ever.

Is the place truly haunted? Or, like perhaps many other great houses in Ireland, does its reputation for ghosts simply arise out of its troubled and turbulent history? And can anything cleanse the place of the dark forces that have always been its portion? Perhaps only time will tell.

MORE BOOKS FROM THE O'BRIEN PRESS

Also by BOB CURRAN

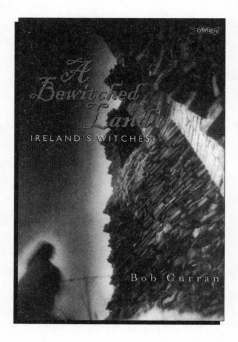

'Curran's meticulously researched book reveals the facts
behind such famous Irish "witches" as Alice Kyteler,
Biddy Early and Moll Anthony.'
SUNDAY WORLD

A BEWITCHED LAND

How did Dame Alice Kyteler escape being burnt as a witch, leaving her unfortunate maidservant to suffer the consequences?

Were Biddy Early and Moll Anthony witches, healers, wise women or charlatans?

And what about the tragic case of Bridget Cleary – was she changeling, witch or victim?

Witch trials in the European or American sense were not common in Ireland although they did occur. In this book the stories of four remarkable court cases that took place from the fourteenth to the nineteenth century are told; other chapters chronicle the extraordinary lives of individuals deemed to be practitioners of the black arts – hedge witches, sorcerers and sinister characters. The book gives a unique insight into the fascinating overlap between witch belief and the vast range of fairy lore that held sway for many centuries throughout the land.

*   *   *

'*A Bewitched Land* is a great read.'
EVENING ECHO

LEGENDARY IRELAND
A Journey Through Celtic Places
and Myths
EITHNE MASSEY

A journey through the places
and legends of ancient Ireland –
a land of warriors, queens, gods
and goddesses. It visits twenty-
eight richly atmospheric sites
and tells their mythological stories, featuring the heroic characters of Celtic lore, such as Cú
Chulainn, Oisín, Diarmuid and
Gráinne. Beautifully illustrated
with haunting photographs and
elegant engravings.

WILD IRISH WOMEN
Extraordinary Lives from History
MARIAN BRODERICK

Writers, killers, artists, nuns,
patriots, healers, pirates, saints,
politicians, eccentrics, entertain-
ers, courtesans, leaders, revolu-
tionaries, lovers, warriors,
witches, record-breakers.

'A fascinating collection of unorthodox women ... This series of lively portraits tells the life stories of 75 women ...
showing that sisters have been doing it for themselves for a
long long time.' BELFAST TELEGRAPH

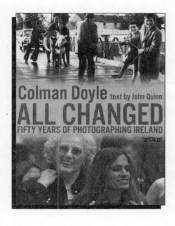

ALL CHANGED
*Fifty Years of
Photographing Ireland*
COLMAN DOYLE
Text by John Quinn

Fifty years of contrast and change,
from the 1950s to today, stun-
ningly captured through the lens
of Ireland's foremost press pho-
tographer, with recollections and
reminiscences by an award-
winning broadcaster and writer.

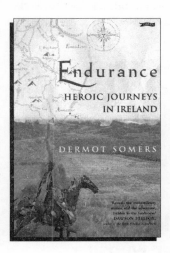

ENDURANCE
Heroic Journeys in Ireland
DERMOT SOMERS

Mountaineer and TV presenter
Dermot Somers follows in the
footsteps of the epic journeys un-
dertaken by legendary figures including Queen Medb, the
Fianna, Brian Boru, Red Hugh
O'Donnell, and O'Sullivan Beare,
exploring the historical periods
and varying landscape revealed by
their amazing travels.

**'The narrative is assured and never laboured ...
apart from the landscape, Somers knows a thing or two
about Irish history'**
SUNDAY TRIBUNE

WAYS OF OLD
Traditional Life in Ireland
OLIVE SHARKEY

Imagine Ireland without tractors,
cars, electricity, running water! This
book brings old Ireland to life with
evocative descriptions of the work,
activities and material possessions of
past generations. Includes superb
black-and-white photographs and
exquisite drawings of the
tools and implements for farming
and ordinary living,
in traditional folk-art style
by the author.

Send for our full-colour catalogue or check out our website

www.obrien.ie